THE PROVENANCE PRESS™
GUIDE TO

THE
WICCAN
YEAR

*Spells, Rituals, and Holiday
Celebrations*

JUDY ANN NOCK

Author of A Witch's Grimoire

Adams Media

New York London Toronto Sydney New Delhi

PROVENANCE
P R E S S

Provenance Press
An Imprint of Simon & Schuster, Inc.
57 Littlefield Street
Avon, Massachusetts 02322

For information about special discounts for bulk purchases, please contact Simon & Schuster Special Sales at 1-866-506-1949 or business@ simonandschuster.com.

The Simon & Schuster Speakers Bureau can bring authors to your live event. For more information or to book an event contact the Simon & Schuster Speakers Bureau at 1-866-248-3049 or visit our website at www. simonspeakers.com.

Interior illustrations by Kathie Kelleher

Manufactured in the United States of America

20 19 18 17 16 15 14

Library of Congress Cataloging-in-Publication Data has been applied for.

ISBN 978-1-59869-125-2

For Jaime,
who has taught me to see the world through new eyes

CONTENTS

Acknowledgments

WE ARE ALL CONNECTED in this web of life, and I am exceedingly grateful to the people who helped make the dream of writing this book a reality. First and foremost, I would like to thank my family, who has seen me through so much and continues to provide unwavering moral support. To my agent, June Clark, my deep appreciation for the tenacity and savvy you exhibited on my behalf. You are a tremendous person and I am lucky to have you in my corner. To my editor, Jennifer Kushnier, your insight and encouragement mean more to me than you can ever know. Your kind words inspired me through many a late night. To Diane Saarinen, I am grateful for your incredible support. To Gabrielle Lichterman, my touchstone, who has been there with me each step of the way; I would not be here without you. You are a true friend and I cherish you. To Arin Murphy-Hiscock, your knowledge has helped give form to a dream. Thank you for your input and insight. To Dr. Ann Gaba and Debby Schwartz, thank you for offering your opinions and advice when I needed it. I have deep respect for your wisdom and experience, and I am fortunate to count you among my friends. To Julie Gillis, Chris Navarro, Galina Krasskova, W. Lyon Martin, and de Traci Regula, thank you for your support of my first book, which paved the way for the second. You have my heartfelt appreciation. I would also like to acknowledge the late Marione Thompson-Helland, editor of *The Beltane Papers*, who passed away in 2006. She gave tremendous support to my first book and she will be missed. And a special thanks to the nine Muses. It has been a pleasure and a great privilege to walk the wheel with you.

Preface

I BEGAN WRITING THIS BOOK on February 2, 2006. Since fate would have me spending the better part of my days chasing an energetic toddler around, most of this book was written at night. Perhaps this is one reason that the book has such a celestial feel to it, as much of it was created under the cloak of midnight with its accompanying inspiring stars. But I would like to offer my readers another explanation as well.

I grew up in a small city in northwest Florida. As a child, I was utterly fascinated by Greek mythology. I consumed every book that I could find on the old myths. While other girls my age wanted to play with their Barbies and pretend to have dates with Ken, I wanted to play Athena and pretend that I had a shield and a magical owl companion. As a teenager, astronomy was one of my favorite hobbies. While my mathematical skills were sorely lacking, I spent many hours stargazing, memorizing constellations, tracking planets, observing the spectacular displays of meteor showers, and identifying roving satellites.

It then occurred to me, once I had the idea to create a book based on the Wiccan wheel of the year, that the night sky has changed very little—imperceptibly, if at all—from the times of the ancient Celts or the Golden Age of Greece. The night sky that I gazed upon in wonder was in fact very much the same as the one that blanketed the builders of Stonehenge.

The earliest of astronomers began recording their observations around 3000 B.C. and hailed from cultures well known for their veneration of the goddess archetypes. In an attempt to make sense out of the universe, these early stargazers were often also priests who linked the placement of the stars to their religion. Early concepts of deity and the constellations were undeniably interwoven; astronomy as well as astrology had deep religious implications. In fact, each of the four major sabbats of the Celtic tradition corresponds to each of the four fixed signs of the zodiac: Samhain occurs under the fixed water sign, Scorpio; Imbolc occurs under the fixed air sign, Aquarius; Beltane occurs under the fixed earth sign, Taurus; and Lughnasad occurs under the fixed fire sign, Leo.

The roots of astronomy as a function of religion date back several thousand years to the earliest Mesopotamian civilizations that are known to be goddess worshippers. The early priest/astronomers of Babylon created the zodiac as a means of dividing the year into twelve segments, establishing one of the earliest known calendars. Consider this excerpt from *Enûma Elish*, the Babylonian genesis myth, as translated by Thorkild Jacobson:

> *"Marduk bade the moon come forth;*
> *Entrusted night to her,*
> *Made her creature of the dark, to measure time;*
> *And every month, unfailingly, adorned her*
> *With a crown."*

Here, the supreme god of creation, Marduk, is credited with establishing the calendar by summoning the lunar goddess. The "crown" he refers to could be a reference to the crescent moon that appears at the beginning and end of each cycle of lunation. Important Egyptian deities such as Isis and Hathor are frequently depicted wearing the horns of the moon as a crown.

The discovery of the Coligny calendar in Bourge, France, in 1897 points to the fact that by A.D. 1, the Celts were using astronomical observation of the lunar cycle to mark the passage of time. This calendar is believed to have been Roman in origin and follows the twenty-eight-day length of the lunar month. The Coligny calendar is of particular significance because there are few documents that survived from ancient Celtic times.

Most Celtic traditions seem to have been passed down orally and survived only in the memories of those who knew them. The earliest written descriptions of Celtic lore are mainly found in the languages of their enemies, the Greeks and Romans. While the Celts were the target of numerous invasions by the Roman Empire, they also enjoyed trade and cultural exchange over several centuries. But unlike the Greeks and Romans, the Celts did not favor temples. Rather, they celebrated their rites in the open air, on hilltops, and among groves of trees with the sky in view.

Additionally, the writings of the Greek poet Hesiod contain many references to the night sky and its role in agriculture. In his tome, *Works and Days*, written around 650 B.C., important dates for beginning planting and harvesting were determined by the rising and setting of certain stars, and by the appearance of specific stars before sunrise or sunset:

> *"When the Pleiades, daughters of Atlas*
> *Are rising,*
> *Begin the harvest, the plowing when they are set.*
> *Forty nights and days they are hidden*
> *And appear again as the year moves round,*
> *When first you sharpen your sickle."*

This is significant because the modern Wiccan wheel of the year has its roots in the old agricultural festivals that marked the beginnings, endings, and culminations of the seasons. While there is no evidence suggesting that any one culture of pre-Christian religious observers enacted all of the festival dates held in the modern Wiccan calendar, there is plenty to suggest that all eight festival days occurred on or near significant events held sacred amongst a variety of cultures and across great distances in time.

Four of the eight sabbats are directly related to the four great Celtic fire festivals, although many will argue that these holidays are specifically Irish and not generally Celtic. Known as the "cross-quarter" days, because they mark the midpoint of the seasons, the festivals of Samhain, Imbolc, Beltane, and Lughnasad are authentically ancient in observation and in name. The four solar festivals of Yule, Ostara, Litha, and Mabon, celebrate the points of change on the celestial equator and are a mix of ancient observances and modern designations. The holidays may be ancient, but the names *Ostara* for the vernal equinox and *Mabon* for the autumnal equinox are modern conventions that gained acceptance and popularity only within the last three decades of the twentieth century. Early Wiccans of the mid-twentieth century did not include the equinox festivals among the sabbats.

Though Wicca is a modern religion, it is based on ancient traditions. The original practitioners of numerous ancient polytheistic religions (many of which inspire the Wicca that is practiced today) used the stars above to mark events that were inextricably tied to how they interpreted and worshipped deity. For example, lunar eclipses were once believed to be caused by the actions of the gods; the appearance of certain stars was interpreted to be ominous or fortuitous.

Many of the same celestial occurrences that guided the builders of stone circles, passage tombs, and temples alike are still readily available to any who wish to observe them. It is for this reason that I encourage readers to become familiar with the stars, as well as their associated myths and legends. They are our most tangible link to the past.

We can look up and see the sky, the same as it was when the first Beltane fire was lit. At Midsummer, we can dance under stars that are still the same as when the festival was originally celebrated in days of old. And we can learn more about the heavens above than the ancient ones could ever have hoped, all the while keeping our sense of wonder and mystery alive. When it seems that everything on Earth has changed, and it feels difficult to conjure the sense of the natural world and our connection to it, we only need to look upwards to know that the moon we see is the same one our ancestors looked to for inspiration.

On a practical note, the seasonal and celestial events described in this book assume that readers are in the northern hemisphere approximately above, on, or below the latitude of 40 degrees North. This would include the United States as well as southern Canada, Europe, central Asia, and Japan. Seasons in the Southern Hemisphere are reversed, and the view of the night sky south of the equator is different from what is described here.

The constellations I have chosen to focus on fall into two groups. There are descriptions of groupings of stars that will be easily visible directly overhead, and there are others that are "dawning"; that is, they are very close to the horizon line and not as easy to see, but their timely appearance directly relates to an occurring sabbat. Additionally, I have endeavored to include information regarding the astrological significance of the zodiac as it pertains to the sabbats. As the *via solis* (the path of the sun) moves through all the constellations of the zodiac that lie along the ecliptic, the energies associated with the constellations can be experienced by the practitioner; however, the constellations will not be readily observable due to the brightness of the sun.

It is my intention with this book to provide readers with relevant information about significant constellations, both when they are visible to the naked eye and when they are invisible, when their influence may still be strongly felt. In order to differentiate what is seen from what is felt, visible constellations are described in respect to their position in the sky along with their prominent stellar features, while constellations lost in the sun's glare are described primarily through their associated traits and implied meanings and myths.

Furthermore, due to an astronomical phenomenon known as precession, the position of the sun against the backdrop of stars has slowly shifted over thousands of years. What we think of today as "sun signs" were actually established thousands of years ago. Today, the dates of the sun's presence within established constellations have changed. Taking precession into account, I have endeavored to include the astrological influences commonly held by tropical astrology, as well as some of the astrological influences of the constellations that the sun is actually in today, where said influences seem relevant. With that said, enjoy your voyage through space and time, and may the glittering jewels of the night attend you. As it is above, so be it below.

Introduction

ON OUR JOURNEY THROUGH LIFE, we may never pass through a single moment more than once. The swift passage of time flows inexorably on. Just as we may never dip our foot into the same river twice as the current moves water to the sea, so too in our many journeys around the sun, we may never experience the same season in quite the same way. The Earth is a great wheel that turns on its axis. The sun is also a great wheel around which the Earth makes its passage. So too can the Earth's ecliptic orbit through the celestial sphere, which encloses the Earth and provides the backdrop against which we view the stars and constellations, be seen as a wheel. These three combined elements encompass the core of what we refer to as the wheel of the year. How similar a year is to a circle! It doesn't take a huge leap of the imagination to equate the 365.25 days of the sidereal year with the 360 degrees of the circle.

There are many ways to acknowledge the passage of time. Whether your observance is simple (as in preparing a special food) or elaborate (such as enacting a ritual), here you will find several appropriate cyclic activities created with the intermediate practitioner in mind. This book is written to inspire and expand your practice as you move through the wheel of the year by providing you with the influences that govern the seasons, meditations that reflect timely themes, and rituals that you may enact in order to enhance your spiritual expression.

The holidays marking the sabbats that we honor today are an amalgamation of many antediluvian rites based on the traditions of various pre-Christian populations, primarily the ancient Greeks, Romans, Celts, and Germanic peoples of northern Europe. Seasons change, and as we acknowledge the precise moment when a solstice or an equinox occurs, we still notice how fluid and rambling the seasons seem to be, flowing into one another so that at times one can scarcely say with any certainty when one ends and another begins. An untimely freeze may occur before an Indian summer day. Early spring teases us just before another blizzard hits. The one constant is unpredictability.

Ancient stone circles of Great Britain and the passage tombs of Ireland attest to the fact that our Celtic predecessors were quite aware of the precise changes that occur along the celestial equator. And although there is little direct evidence that the Celts celebrated the solar cycles of solstices and equinoxes, we know for certain that they were aware of them because they did celebrate the precise moments in between.

Meanwhile, in Rome, the winter solstice was celebrated during the festivities of the Saturnalia, while the Greeks observed the Eleusinian mysteries during the autumnal equinox. We may now have more sophisticated and scientific language to describe these natural occurrences of solar and planetary alignment, but we are no less mystified by the subtle as well as amplified energy experienced during these times.

The sacred descent and resurrection of the goddess is an allegory for the journey of the Earth around the sun. The pivotal stations of her sacred cycle are birth, initiation, consummation, descent, death, and rebirth. It is this life cycle, expressed through the changing seasons, that we celebrate through the wheel of the year. We can align our practice with the planetary energies by first becoming conscious of the changes as they are occurring.

Take a moment to look around and capture a moment in time. Your observations will create awareness. Invent bold new traditions based on ancient rites. This is part of the beauty of Wicca. There is no orthodox liturgy to which to adhere. Your observances can be as fluid as the tides and as creative as you are able to dream. Empower your rituals with newfound knowledge. Celebrate your individual relationship to the Earth by taking a step on the sacred spiral path. Dare to name that which you call Goddess. The great mother of all creation is calling to you with the gentle breezes of spring, the fresh rain of summer, the chill of autumn, and the silence of winter. The primeval mother is beckoning you forth from your sleep of dreams to imagine a new reality where intention bonds with action, and action with repetition.

This is the essence of tradition: spiritual expressions grounded through clear intentions and repeated on auspicious days at carefully chosen times so that we may attune with the power of the changing Earth and allow this power to transform our lives. Her magic is inspiration, and inspiration will guide you as you deepen yourself to the path of the goddess. Come. Take a step. Time waits for no one. The Great Wheel is turning, and a magical journey awaits you.

Season One

SAMHAIN
A YEAR ENDS, A YEAR BEGINS

OUR JOURNEY BEGINS on October 31 with Samhain, the witch's New Year and the midpoint between the autumnal equinox and the winter solstice. The word *samhain* is Irish, meaning "summer's end." Samhain represents the third and final harvest of the year, where the remaining produce is stored to provide nourishment during the coming winter. In addition to the storing of winter provisions, Samhain had agricultural significance in other ways. In Ireland, it was the day on which pigs were killed and when cattle were moved from the mountains into protected pastures for the winter.

The identification of Samhain with the beginning of the New Year comes from the Celtic tradition of each day beginning at sundown. Just as each sabbat festival begins on the eve of the celebrated day, so too does the year begin with the advent of winter. In addition to archaeology, early Irish accounts suggest that Samhain was also a festival when alcoholic beverages were consumed. Several great legends that include references to intoxication are all said to have occurred on Samhain. Among them are the Féis Temro inauguration of kings and the Adventure of Nera. Remnants of wine- or ale-making equipment have been unearthed, but curiously, no accompanying storage vessels like those often found in Greece. This suggests that the harvest grain was fermented and then consumed throughout the Samhain season.

On Samhain night, it is believed that the dead walk and that faeries cavort, causing both magic and mayhem. In Ireland, a great bonfire was lit on the hill of Tlachtga, which was the funeral site for the progeny of Partholón, one of the first divinities of the land. Samhain is the time of the Cailleach, the crone who rules the winter season. Offerings and sacrifices were made in her honor.

THE FEAST OF SAMHAIN

Because the climate of the seasons was once so difficult to predict, Samhain was a celebration of bounty but also a time of fear. No matter how much preparation was done, one could never be sure what was to come or whether the provisions for winter would be sufficient. Oftentimes, an early frost was interpreted as otherworldly spirits blighting the vegetation with their breath. This type of "weather as omen" belief may have given rise to the notion of dead spirits cavorting about and faeries plotting to steal away human beings on Samhain night.

In faerie lore, Samhain is the night of the "wild hunt," a notorious and rambunctious ride when scores of faeries come racing out from within their hollow hills to wreak havoc throughout the towns. Meandering mortals avoided traversing near the *sidhe*, or faerie mounds, out of fear of abduction. And if one did venture out during the wild hunt, it was only under the auspices of a protective charm, such as salt or iron. Turning one's clothing inside out was another way to protect against faerie mischief. Faerie lore claims that a stone with a natural hole through it, dry but found near the water, would enable the wearer to enter the faerie realm and return from it unharmed. This same type of amulet was also believed to protect horses from faerie mischief and theft.

Perhaps it was the practice of wearing charms for protection that led Samhain to become a night for divination. Many different methods of divination were used by the Celts in order for young girls to learn the name of a future husband. Others sought to get a glimpse of the future and obtain information about a future occupation. Some of the techniques they used included burning nuts in the hearth fire and making assumptions based upon which nuts exploded and which did not; pouring molten lead into cool water, then interpreting the shapes that formed in order to get clues about a future occupation; and the baking of *soddag valloo*, or "dumb cakes," a Manx Gaelic custom involving cakes, which were baked directly on top of the embers of the fire. Eating the cake in silence was thought to encourage prophetic dreams in young women seeking to learn the identity of their future husbands, provided that they left the room without turning their backs on the fire. Babies born on Samhain were thought to possess divinatory power and were often treated with special respect as well as fear.

Samhain is also the time when rituals were held to honor the dead. Benevolent spirits were beckoned and tempted with favorite foods that they enjoyed during life. Malevolent spirits were banished and kept away. The origin of the jack o' lantern is rooted in the belief of wandering spirits and ghosts. The lantern's glow was meant as a beacon for the spirits of the dearly departed, while the terrible faces carved therein were meant to frighten away any spirit with ill intentions.

Celestial Events
PHOENIX AND PEGASUS

The autumn equinox has long passed, and the sun makes its journey south along the ecliptic, spending less and less time above the horizon. The approach of winter is palpable now. There is a chill in the air, and the days are noticeably shorter. If you are brave enough to venture out on Samhain night, and if it is a moonless night, you will find an enchanting array of stars emblazoned across the celestial sphere.

Rising along the southern horizon, Phoenix, an obscure constellation, spreads its wings into the night sky around 10:00 P.M. Although the constellation will never fully rise in the Northern Hemisphere, most of it can be seen only at Samhain, remaining true to its elusive mythological nature. It is also a significant

Samhain observation, as the phoenix is a symbol of death and rebirth. Search the sky along the horizon directly south (appropriately enough, the direction associated with elemental fire), to find Phoenix rising. The bright star Fomalhaut (part of the constellation Piscis) serves as your guide. Just above the treetops, Fomalhaut will be above and to the right of Phoenix's wings.

The phoenix, a mythical bird that rises from its own ashes once every 500 years, is self-created through parthenogenesis and is said to complete the cycle of death and rebirth through fire. It is described as a gigantic bird with resemblances to the peacock, pheasant, and eagle, with a prominent crest and spectacular plumage that includes all the colors of the rainbow. An extraordinarily gentle creature, the phoenix is said to feed only on air, which incidentally is also the food of fire. Descriptions of the phoenix appear in several different mythologies, Egyptian, Greek, and Mesopotamian among them. In Egypt, the phoenix is called Bennu and is depicted in hieroglyphs as a heron-like bird. Sacred to Osiris and Ra, the Bennu makes its home inside the obelisk and represents resurrection and the morning star. Its ashes are said to ignite in Heliopolis upon the altar within the temple of the sun. Varying accounts say the Greek historian Hesiod observed the living phoenix, while other versions claim that he never did see the bird, but that its fantastic reputation inspired him to include references to it in his writing.

The Window of Pegasus

The phoenix is not the only mythical winged creature that appears in the sky at this time. One of the most spectacular and

5

easy-to-recognize constellations in autumn is Pegasus, the winged horse. Around 10:00 P.M. on calendrical Samhain, October 31, the Great Square of Pegasus will be very close to the zenith (the point directly overhead). Pegasus is visible when facing south and is characterized by four second-magnitude stars. These four stars—Alpheratz, Sheat, Algenib, and Markab—make up the central "window" that is this constellation's most recognizable feature. On a clear night in the city, the window of Pegasus is easily spotted, but on a clear and moonless night in the country, that same window reveals dozens of stars. Looking through the window of Pegasus is akin to looking back through time. What you are actually seeing is the edge of our galaxy, and all of the history that it contains. The light of the stars you are seeing has traveled billions of miles through space to reach your eyes.

Pegasus appears in several myths of the Greek pantheon as an invaluable ally to conquering heroes. Some versions claim Pegasus was created from Medusa's blood when Perseus killed the Gorgon. Perseus rode Pegasus when he rescued Andromeda from the sacrificial rock. She was chained as an offering to Poseidon's monster so that her death could atone for her mother's vanity. Pegasus appears again as an aid to Bellerophon in the killing of the Chimera.

Pegasus is a bringer of inspiration. The sacred spring of Hippocrene on the mountain of Helicon, home of the Muses, was created where his hoof struck the earth. Allow the magic of Pegasus to inspire you as you gaze through the window of his body. Reflect on your own sacred origin and know that these images, too, are right now traveling through the fabric of space.

Keep in mind that both the phoenix and Pegasus are winged creatures. Allow your imagination to take flight, be bold, and feel free to reinvent yourself at this time.

The Tragic and Joyful Maiden and Mother

The constellation Andromeda shines almost directly from the zenith point on Samhain night. The window of Pegasus will lead you eastward to her chains, an eternal reminder of her near-sacrifice to the sea monster Cetus and of Perseus's daring rescue. Daughter of the Ethiopian queen Cassiopeia, Andromeda and her narrowly avoided fate stand as a reminder of the wrath of the deities when a mortal claims superiority. The vanity of Cassiopeia was evident in her claim that her daughter was more beautiful than the daughters of the sea god. And although Andromeda was innocent, the wrath of the gods lay on her head instead of her mother's.

Depicted by her signature throne, Cassiopeia lies to the north of Andromeda and Pegasus. Her constellation appears as a giant "W" if you are facing north and conversely, an "M" if you are facing south. The ancient Britons referred to the Cassiopeia constellation as Llys Dôn, or Dôn's Court. The goddess Dôn is believed to be the British counterpart to the Gaelic Danu, the mother of all gods. The throne is also one of the more prevalent symbols of the Egyptian goddess Isis, who rescues her husband from death. The legend of Andromeda concerns salvation from a death sentence and freedom from bondage, and the resurrection of Osiris represents triumph over actual death, symbolism that is especially poignant at Samhain.

Meditation
PHOENIX RISING

As we honor the dead on Samhain, it is important to acknowledge
the intensity of emotion that comes with confronting death. Use
this meditation if you are confronting grief or another emotional
situation that requires insight and compassion. Sit comfortably
and close your eyes. Ground and center your energy. Breathe
rhythmically as you imagine yourself in a topiary garden, standing among tall hedges.

● Beneath your feet is the soft earth, blanketed with the tender green of lush grass. You wander among carefully trimmed
bushes with leaves so dense that you cannot see through the
hedges. They are unusually tall, and you cannot see over them.
You cannot tell where one ends and another begins. It is as if living walls surround you.

● You take cautious steps along a turning path that does
not seem to end. Time feels suspended. Each step could be a
hundred steps, and you feel as though you have been wandering
far too long. If you have made any progress at all finding your
way out, it is indiscernible.

● You feel lost and confused, each new direction looking
exactly like the turn that preceded it. You begin to feel that you
will never leave this garden. Although it is beautiful, it is too
overwhelming because your feelings of uncertainty and loss are
dominant.

● Suddenly, above your head you feel a cool breeze that gradually begins to strengthen in its intensity. Your heart begins to pound, so loud that it seems to be outside of yourself. You then realize that the sound is not coming from within your own body, but rather from the wind that you feel above your head.

● You turn your gaze upwards and are amazed to learn that the sound and the wind are the beating of powerful wings. Above you flies the form of a creature, the likes of which you have never seen. It is a bird! A fantastic bird, so large that the gigantic hedge seems no more than a tiny perch beneath the great expanse of its wings.

● From its majestic wingspan, the mighty flight feathers project with a multitude of shining opalescent hues. You see brilliant blues iridescent with shades of rose and violet. Your eyes follow this amazing display of color to the soft down feathers at the base of the wings. They appear velvety and are a deep royal purple. Elegant curling plumage like that of a bird of paradise extends to the scarlet tail feathers.

● Your jaw drops, and the creature alights on the top of the hedge and cranes its graceful neck, folding in its wings and bringing its face very close to yours. In its golden beak, you see the radiance of the sun itself. The metallic color blends in with the delicate feathers of its face that range from shimmering gold to a shining yellow. On its crest, you can see deep reds that change to bright orange and rosy pinks. But you are most struck by the eye of the phoenix. It looks at you so intently with eyes the color of the Mediterranean Sea; the irises are clear bright blue and watery, the pupils, only a slightly darker blue.

9

You are awestruck and mesmerized by its eyes. You begin to see reflections appear, and you know it is because this gentle creature is feeling the uncertainty in your soul, and reflecting this back to you with kindness and compassion.

You see familiar images, as if you are gazing into a pool of blessed water. Faces of loved ones. People who have helped you in the past. Tender memories that you had once forgotten now come alive. The phoenix meets your gaze and sheds a glistening tear. The tear falls over you and you are bathed in a fragrant aspersion of comforting empathy. You realize that the phoenix is feeling what you feel.

On some level, in your distress you have summoned the phoenix to come to your aid, and indeed it has. Carefully, it lifts you on to its mighty back and spreads its shimmering wings. Together, you soar upwards through the clear blue sky, the winds of change touching your face causing tears of joy and release to stream from your eyes. You turn your head to look down.

Beneath you, you see the labyrinth that you previously stumbled through, only now from your lofty vantage, you can easily see the way out. You are free of the maze and its resolution is obvious.

Unexpectedly and without warning, you are standing in the garden once again. The phoenix is high overhead and you squint your eyes against the glare of the sun. It becomes more and more difficult to see as the sun seems to shine brighter and brighter until the fantastic bird is no longer discernible at all.

You can barely see its outline against the sun when suddenly it seems to erupt in a fireball so large and bright that it makes the light of the accompanying sun seem pale in comparison. You shield your eyes and turn away, but the image seems burned into your retinas. Every time you blink, you see the phoenix.

The sensation begins to fade a little, and you take your first steps. You are confident and reassured now. Every few steps, you see the light of the phoenix behind your eyes. You understand that this light is leading you along the pathway out of the labyrinth. You simply follow it. You are on your way home.

Ritual
SET YOURSELF FREE

Remembering Andromeda's narrow escape, use the energy and inspiration of the stars to break through your own psychic bondage and release yourself from figurative chains that may be holding you back. Samhain is an ideal time for taking an inventory of life and releasing old patterns that may no longer prove useful. Start by gathering your tools. You will need these things:

11

A *ball of red yarn*
Athalme
Cauldron
Matches

1. Take a ball of red cotton yarn or thread and cut it into nine-inch pieces. It is important that you choose a natural substance for this exercise. Avoid synthetics like acrylic or polyester.

2. As you knot the ends of each piece of yarn together, forming a circle, give each one a name, something in your life that you feel is holding you back. Perhaps it is a past hurt that you have been dwelling on. Maybe you have some regrets in life. Whether it is pain or grief or regret that binds you, it is now time to lay these down. It takes a certain kind of strength to carry a burden, but an even greater strength to cast it away.

3. Use as many or as few pieces as you need. Put them around your wrist and tell them specifically, "_____, I have carried you long and far. Your burden has been my teacher, and I accept your lessons. Now I summon the strength to release you, for your presence serves me no longer."

4. Take your athalme and begin cutting through the circlets. As the blade is invariably dull, this will be no easy task. Be persistent, and as you cut away your symbolic bonds, imagine yourself separating from your actual bonds. Nothing worth doing is ever easy, and this small struggle is representative of something much greater: the individual, which is you, accepting responsibility and influence over the events of life, which is magic.

5. When your bonds have been cut, burn them in your cauldron, saying, "I send you back to the dark mother, to be consumed by the flames of transformation. You are purified and changed forever in this fire, reduced to your pure and simple essence. You are no longer bound to me. I send you back to the mother, and away you will go, that something new and blessed in me shall grow."

6. When the flames subside and the cauldron cools, gather the ashes in a small pot and take them outside. Determine which way the wind is blowing and stand with the wind at your back. Blow the ashes into the air. Let them dissipate and vanish. Prepare yourself to make a new start.

Astrological Influences
THE REIGN OF SCORPIO AND THE AGE OF INTROSPECTION

In tropical astrology, the sun enters Scorpio on October 24, and this influence is surely felt at Samhain. The eighth sign of the zodiac, Scorpio's symbology is extremely complex. It is the only sign with three representative symbols: the scorpion, the snake, and the eagle. Along with the fiery passion that this sun sign evokes, Scorpio is associated with death more than any other sign. Ancient Mesopotamian mythology describes the gates of the underworld as being guarded by scorpion men.

The goddess most closely associated with Scorpio is the maiden huntress Artemis. In Greek mythology, Artemis is the daughter of Zeus, the father of the gods, and Leto. She is also the twin sister of Apollo, the god of the sun. Artemis is the goddess of the moon and of the hunt. Her cult in Greece was connected to the female transformations of birth, puberty, and death.

In her lunar association, she is the protector of all the nocturnal animals of the forest and is attended by women only. She is merciless in her defense of her virginal status and is a lethal foe to any man who affronts her. Legends tell of Artemis calling forth a gigantic scorpion that she unleashes on the hunter

13

Orion, killing him. Variations of the myth propose many different reasons for the slaying. Some say it was jealousy that drove
Artemis to send the scorpion after Orion; Orion was a threat
to her power as goddess of the hunt if his skills were thought
to rival her own. Other versions of the tale cast Artemis as the
defending maiden, killing Orion in self-defense to avoid rape
and the loss of her virginity. A third version suggests that Orion
was too successful a hunter, and Artemis feared for her beloved
animals on Earth, thinking that Orion would kill them all and
sought only to protect them from the danger he presented. As a
reward for killing Orion, Artemis placed the scorpion in the sky
where it is visible today as the brilliant constellation Scorpius.

At the time of Samhain, the sun is in Scorpius, and so the
stars are not readily visible to the stellar observer. Rather, look
for the constellation Scorpius to make its dramatic appearance
in the summer sky. Scorpius is one of the few constellations that
closely resembles the animal that it represents. The red-giant
star Antares is the eye of the scorpion, while the double star
Shaula is the stinger. One story of Shaula tells of two children, a
brother and sister, who flee to the sky to escape an abusive par-
ent and forever find refuge in the heavens.

The snake, another symbol of Scorpio, has an equally complex symbology. While often regarded in the West as a symbol
of evil, elsewhere throughout the world the snake represents
wisdom and regenerative power. Because the snake sheds its
skin during molting, it is looked upon as a symbol of life, death,
and rebirth. The ouroborous, which depicts a snake consuming
its own tail, has long been regarded as a potent magical symbol

of inspiration, renewal, and the eternal cycle of nature. It is an embodiment of eternity.

The eagle of Scorpio represents the evolved soul and has correlations with the phoenix as well. The eagle is sometimes viewed as a form of Artemis herself. In Greek mythology, gods and goddesses frequently take on the form of animals for a variety of reasons, most often to interact with mortals while concealing their divine identity.

A fixed water sign, Scorpio is also a negative sign in the sense that signs carry a positive or negative charge. In traditional astrology, the negative signs are believed to project predominantly feminine energy, while the positive signs are associated with masculine energy. It is ruled by Pluto and correlates with the age of introspection due to its placement on the zodiac. If one imagines that a soul must incarnate as a different astrological sign at each rebirth in order to fully evolve, then Scorpio represents that place in a soul's evolution where the cumulative effects of all previous lifetimes are taken into account and examined. This is especially significant in its relationship to Samhain, as this time of year is an excellent time for taking an inventory of life, discarding the superfluous, and making positive changes.

Legends and Lore: The Story of Tam Lin

In English and Scottish legend, Tam Lin is a handsome young knight who captured the fancy of the Faerie Queen. During a near-fatal accident, in which he is thrown from his horse, the Faerie Queen intervenes by kidnapping him and thus preventing his untimely death. She imprisons him inside a well in Carterhaugh, where he remains in an odd state of limbo.

Tam Lin seduces young girls who are overcome by his attractiveness once they summon him by pulling on a double rose that grows beside the well, but he is unable to leave its confines. He falls in love with Janet, a visiting maiden, whom he impregnates. He implores her to come to his aid and release him from the spell of the Faerie Queen whom he fears plans to forsake him to hell. In this excerpt from a popular version of the ballad by Francis James Child, Tam Lin gives Janet a lively description of the wild hunt and the potency of faerie magic as well as the actions required to break the spell:

"But the night is Halloween, lady,
The morn is Hallowday,
Then win me, win me, an ye will,
For well I want ye may.

"Just at the dark and midnight hour
The fairy folk will ride,
And they that would their true-love win,
At Miles Cross they must bide."

"But how shall I thee know, Tam Lin,
Or how my true-love know,
Among so many strange knights,
The like I never saw?"

"O first let pass the black, lady,
And then let pass the brown,
But quickly run to the milk-white steed,
Pull ye his rider down.

"For I'll ride on the milk-white steed,
And nearest to the town,
Because I was an earthly knight
They give me that renown.

"My right hand will be gloved, lady,
My left hand will be bare,
Tilted up shall my hat be,
And combed down shall my hair.
And that's the token I give thee,
No doubt I will be there.

"They'll turn me in your arms, lady,
Into an newt or a snake,
But hold me fast, and fear me not,
I am your baby's father.

"They'll turn me to a bear so fierce,
And then a lion bold,
But hold me fast, and fear me not,
And ye shall love your child.

"Again they'll turn me in your arms
To a red hot brand of iron,
But hold me fast, and fear me not,
I'll do you no harm.

"And last they'll turn me in your arms
Into the burning gleed,
Then throw me into well water,
O throw me in with speed.

"And then I'll be your own true-love,
I'll turn into a naked knight,
Then cover me with your green mantle,
And hide me out of sight."

One of the more interesting aspects of this excerpt is the reference to the occult significance of water. Before Tam Lin can once again return to human form, he must first pass through a stand of water in order to break the enchantment of the faeries.

Meditation
DESCEND TO THE REALM OF HECATE

In this trance journey through the deep earth, you will discover the realm of Hecate, the Crone Goddess of Wisdom. She is the dark face of the goddess, and many fear her. It is Hecate who attends women in childbirth, and it is she whom we will face at the end of our life's journey. Take this opportunity to name and face your fear. Is it advanced age? Death? To create positive change, you must honor her with respect to receive her blessing and aid.

18

● You are standing in a vast and empty field. The last of the harvest has been cut and gathered and stands drying in the barn. In the distance, an orchard of apple trees stands fruitless, save for the last few fallen apples of the season that rest on the ground as if the very wind has made an offering to the earth mother.

● You face the setting sun, which sinks lower in the sky, illuminating the painted leaves that rush by. A strong wind from the east is at your back, and the tumultuous journey of the swirling leaves echoes a feeling from deep within your soul.

● You feel the earth start to tremble. It is as if you are standing on a fault line and the tectonic plates have begun to shift. You experience a sense of exhilaration, as if a mighty change is about to occur. Your intuition proves to be absolutely correct.

● You watch in amazement as the earth opens before you. What began as a rumble, then a crack emanating from the very place where you stand, turns into a deep chasm. You peer inside, noticing the vast network of roots still clinging to the earth from stalks long since cut.

● You take a step into the gap in the earth. You notice small tunnels made by burrowing insects and small animals. A family of chipmunks huddles together, bracing for the coming cold. You feel no fear, only curiosity as to the secrets of the dark earth.

● You are compelled to go further. You step carefully, loosened rocks tumbling on ahead to unseen realms. You notice the colorful striations in the rocks as you descend. Pockets in the matrix reveal glittering crystals, so perfectly formed they look as though they had been deliberately placed along your path.

19

● Light begins to fade as the surface of the Earth retreats into the distance, but you forge ahead, led by the sensation that a great mystery is being revealed to you. You feel the pulsating rhythms of the Earth itself and a great truth is affirmed for you. The earth is alive and teeming with life. As it is above, so it is below.

● You are enveloped in the darkness, when, strangely, you begin to perceive a light. This seems as strange and fantastic as the journey you are presently undertaking. The faint light of a gently glowing ember guides you along your path until you find yourself unexpectedly facing a woman. Her hair is long and white, and her face is etched with the songs and stories of a thousand lifetimes. You recognize her instantly. She is the grandmother of all, the ancient crone of your imaginings.

● You stop and stand before her in awe. At her feet is a large black cauldron. Beneath the cauldron is the fire that led you to her. Without speaking, her voice appears in your mind and she asks you why you have come to her. You reply, "I seek to learn the mysteries of the earth and to honor you with respect."

● She nods and stirs the cauldron and asks, "Who are you?" You pause because you know her question is more profound than it seems. She is not asking your name. She is asking you to name the desire of your soul, to make a connection between yourself and the divine, to acknowledge yourself as an integral part of the earth you have chosen to penetrate and explore.

● You answer wordlessly, "I do not know." She stops stirring the cauldron and bids you to gaze into its depths. You do not know the liquid that it contains, but it swirls around as though she was still stirring it.

● You see your own face reflected on the surface, and as the surface churns, your appearance begins to change. You see yourself as a very young person, full of energy and vitality. Then the image begins to change again before your eyes. You see yourself as a mature person, fulfilled and happy.

● Another spiral sweeps this vision from your eyes and you are revealed this time as an old person with the light of a lifetime dancing in your eyes. You look up into the eyes of the crone and you hear a voice inside your head. You are not certain if it is your own voice or that of the manifestation of the goddess before you, but you cannot argue with its message:

"I am the Maiden, seeker of Wisdom."
"I am the Mother, giver of Wisdom."
"I am the Crone, keeper of Wisdom."

● You understand that this truth has been revealed to you through the woman standing before you. She is the woman you will one day become, just as surely as the reflections in her dark cauldron are aspects of yourself as well. By approaching her with honor and respect instead of fear, you have enabled your- self to embody this truth and you know it is now time for you to leave the underground realm of darkness and mystery.

● You now realize that in the span of your own lifetime, however long or short, you have already learned many things, taught many things, and have much still to learn. As the maiden, you learned how to navigate through all of life. You began life as a helpless infant and learned independence. At the same time, you taught your parents how to nurture and ultimately how to let go. As the mother, you nurtured dreams of your own and shared your wisdom with others. As the crone, most of your lifetime lies behind you. You own all of your achievements, triumphs, and trials. And there is still more that you desire from life. You have already died and been reborn many times within this one lifetime.

21

With this realization, you face her one last time. Her visage vanishes before your eyes, as does her cauldron and its reassuring glow. You are alone and standing in near-total darkness, yet you feel a comforting warmth about your shoulders. You turn around and see that the glowing embers that lit the cauldron have been replaced by the waning rays of the setting sun, seemingly miles away, dancing on the surface of the Earth as you remain far beneath.

You begin the slow ascent back up to the surface of the world. You pass by the glittering gems hidden deep within the matrix, a tangible testament to the power of change. Years of pressure and temperature changes have yielded something unique and beautiful in a purely natural state, a treasure meant for your eyes alone.

You climb higher and notice again the colorful striations in the compacted soil and marvel at the intricate network of deep roots that penetrate the dark earth, as complex and thick and sturdy as any oak branch that weaves its way through the sky. The earth is living all around you, home to insects and small animals and all kinds of plants, forming delicate connections never seen by light of day or by the light of the moon.

You emerge just as the sun makes its final descent below the horizon, bathing the field in the magical purples of twilight. The brightest stars are becoming visible now. You notice that the wind has shifted and now blows from the west.

You smile as you stand among the swirling leaves that come rushing towards you. Your change has come.

Ritual

REMEMBERING THE DEAD

Samhain was a traditional time for honoring the dead among the Celts. Those who welcomed the departed spirits would set out a meal for them. Many considered the visiting dead to be friendly and welcomed their presence with respect and a noted absence of fear. For this ritual, you will need these things:

> *Photos or images of departed loved ones*
> *Other mementos, objects, or reminders to place on the altar*
> *Special foods that departed loved ones enjoyed in life*
> *Candles*
> *Pomegranate and apples*
> *Chalice with wine or fruit juice*
> *Sage or incense*

Take a moment to ground and center your energy. You can do this by practicing deep-breathing exercises and burning a little of your favorite incense. Adorn your altar with photographs and other tokens of loved ones who have died. Set out apples and pomegranates, the fruits of the season, as an offering to the goddess. Darken the room; let it be illuminated only by candles. Do a brief purification ritual, such as a smudging ceremony, and call the quarters. You may invoke the directions in this manner:

> *"I call upon the spirits of the eastern realm, the ethereal wind whose invisible and unseen form is known by the movement it*

creates. Kind spirits, travel on the winds of fate to enter into this temple. You are most welcome here on this night of nights."

"I call upon the spirits of the southern realms, the fire that consumes the phoenix. Through death we are reborn. Through fire we are purified until nothing but our original and untainted essence remains. The fire of the spirit may change, but it may never be extinguished. Familiar spirits, I beckon you towards the candles' glow. Enter into this temple tonight. You are most welcome here."

"I call upon the spirits of the western realm, the deep mysteries of the water. Beloved spirits, many tears I have shed at your passing from this realm. By the water that is my blood, I ask for your presence here tonight. Sail upon the sea of mystery and enter into this temple. You are most welcome."

"I call upon the spirits of the northern realm, the mighty earth. Divine earth spirit, who cradles the bones of the dead, I bid you reveal the mysteries that you contain. The earth that I walk upon and adore is the same earth that houses the remains of my beloveds and the bones of my ancestors. I ask for your blessing as you descend into this temple. Gentle spirits of the earth, you are most welcome here."

24

Since Samhain is a sabbat of great power where spirits are known to be in contact and communication with the earthly realm, it would behoove you to do a protection spell or speak a charm banishing any unwanted guests and preventing unwelcome spirits from entering into your sacred space:

"Elemental spirits, protect me that no harm may come to me, nor to my beloveds! Spirits of air, blow hard and strong that all

*evil may disappear and be gone. Spirits of fire, may you burn so
bright that malevolence is consumed in your brilliant light. Spirits
of water, your power can drown. May wickedness never dare to
come 'round. May the spirits of earth with their strength and their
starkness stand between me and the agents of darkness!"*

● Invoke Hecate or a goddess from a pantheon with which
you resonate that embodies the crone aspect, for this is her time.

● Choose a comfortable sitting position and think of all
your beloveds who have passed on to life beyond the veil. Say
their names aloud. Tell their stories. Speak the dates of their
births and of their deaths.

● Let the memories wash over you like waves of the ocean.
Remember the things that they enjoyed in this life. What were
their favorite foods, or their favorite music? Partake of these
things yourself to honor their lives and to strengthen your connection to them. Death does not end a relationship, but it can
certainly make communication more difficult, especially for
those that do not possess the talents of the spiritual medium.

25

● Say aloud things you have left unsaid. Do not feel shame or
sorrow. You can be sure that tonight, the spirits are listening.

● Turn your focus onto your own lineage. Think back until
you can see your nearest relatives who are deceased. They may be
your parents, your grandparents, or your great-grandparents.

● Picture your ancestors in your mind. It does not matter
if you do not have a photographic image of them or a clear idea
of what they may have looked like. Close your eyes and breathe
and ask them to make themselves known to you.

● Trust the images that come to you as coming from them. Let them know that you are seeking them out, welcoming them into your home with honor and remembrance.

● Imagine what their lives may have been like, what sacrifices they must have made for you to be in the place where you are now. Think of the lands that they traveled across and picture the landscape as it might have been during their lifetime.

● Think about how the actions of distant people far across time in another land have shaped your reality and the world as you know it today. Take a journey in your mind. Imagine what brought your ancestors to the choices that they made in life. Who preceded them? What continent did they originate from?

● Follow this thread as far back as it will take you. Open your mind to possibilities and let your imagination guide you. Allow yourself to trace your line even further until you are able to imagine the creation of Earth itself.

● Follow your connection to your ultimate origin from primordial Earth to the cosmos. Know that we are all one, that all life is interconnected and that death is not an end, but an awakening into a new reality and a continuation of our spiritual evolution.

● Let your candles burn down late into the night. Watch as the wax drips, pools, and then cools. Allow yourself to grieve for the separation that death creates, but remember that death is not the end. Just as matter cannot be created or destroyed, but merely changes from one state to another, believe that it is much the same for your corporeal body, which is but a temporary home for your undying spirit. Shakespeare so eloquently described death as "a sea change into something rich and strange."

● Bask in the presence of your departed friends. Embrace the memories of family long gone once again. This is their night. Welcome the echoes of voices long ago silenced into your mind.

● Raise a chalice in their honor and enjoy the things they loved while on earth. Pour a libation into the earth, or into a houseplant as the case may be. Acknowledge the changing times. The harvested fields are reaped and lay barren as winter's grip begins to take hold. The veil between the worlds is very thin, and the faeries make their presence known.

● Cut a segment of your pomegranate. Peel off some of the white skin and place a few of the seeds upon your pentacle or another small dish upon your altar. Hold your hands over the seeds and give them a blessing, such as this one:

"How brief is the beauty of the fruitful earth. Her time of flowers and fruits now comes to an end. In the name of the radiant Maiden and Queen of the Underworld, Persephone, I welcome the coming darkness."

Samhain Charm

In your mortar and pestle, combine equal parts of pine (needles or resin), clove buds, and dried ginger root. Grind them together into a fine powder. Place the mixture in the center of a three-inch round piece of black felt. Gather up the edges and tie them closed with a red thread. Wear this herbal charm on your person, or keep it in your pocket. The pine will deflect evil, while the clove is sacred to Hecate, and the ginger is an offering to the dead.

● Eat the seeds and share them with your companions, should there be any present.

● Extinguish your candles and release the directions. Open the circle and give thanks to the goddesses invoked. Sleep and have enchanted dreams of benevolent visiting spirits.

Practical Craft
CARVING A MAGICAL O'LANTERN

The original jack-o-lanterns were carved out of turnips and cabbages. The carving of pumpkins, gourds, and other fruits of the harvest season is still in wide practice today. Although this has survived as a secular tradition and is now part of the fun of the Halloween celebration, it can take on a much greater significance. You will need these things:

1 medium pumpkin	*Medium bowl*
Felt tip pen	*Votive candle or tea light*
Bolline	*Toothpicks*
Newspaper	*Long kitchen matches*
Large spoon	

28

Meditate on the symbol of the pentagram, for its use here will be twofold. The pentagram when viewed upright has many connotations. In this ritual, it will be used as a symbol of protection. The inverted pentagram is frequently subjected to controversial associations, and for this reason it is not often used.

While the inverted pentagram is a symbol of undeniable power and often brings with it a sense of fear, in this exercise, we will look at the inverted pentagram in a new way. As you meditate on the upright pentagram and its protective associations, think of it as a shield, deflecting any unwanted and unwelcome influences. When you view the pentagram in its inverted position, think of it as a channel or conduit through which benevolent energy may pass. One way to visualize this dual power of the pentagram is to imagine the point of the star at the top as an impenetrable psychic weapon against undesired energy. It is the proverbial athalme against which those spirits that enter without love or trust must fall. When turned upside down, imagine the pentagram to be a doorway; between the two uppermost points of the star is the veil between the worlds through which the spirits you invoke may pass. The purpose of the magical lantern is to ward off unwanted spirits, while at the same time acting as a beacon for those with whom we wish to visit us on Samhain night. The dual use of the pentagram is to take advantage of both of its associations so that it may function as a portal as well as a shield.

Use the knife to carve the pentagram directly onto the top of the candle. You should use the entire edge of the knife, not just the tip. Lay the blade across the candle surface so that the wick is in the center of the knife. Your first cut will be from the upper right to the bottom center, then from the bottom center to the upper left, from the upper left to the right (centered), from right to left (centered), and finally from left to the upper right, making an inverted pentagram.

After you have placed the invoking pentagram onto your candle you may bless and dress the candle and set it on your altar. Since the candle is small and its symbolism powerful, some essential oil (pine or garlic, for warding off evil) and powdered incense will suffice for candle dressing. A simple charm can be spoken:

"May my beloveds from beyond the veil
Follow your gentle glowing light.
Illuminate their journey
On this sacred night of nights."

Now prepare your pumpkin by thoroughly washing and drying its surface. Spread out the newspapers and place the pumpkin on top of them and keep the bowl handy. Using the pen, draw an octagon around the stem of the pumpkin. This will be your guide for cutting the top. You want to draw the octagon so that there is plenty of room between the cuts and the stem, but not so large that it encroaches upon the sides—the octagon should not be seen when you view the pumpkin from its side.

Place the tip of the knife at the edge of one of the lines of the octagon and press it directly into the pumpkin at an approximate 20-degree angle pointing towards the center of the pumpkin. Remove the knife and repeat this all around the octagon. By cutting at an inward angle instead of straight down, you are ensuring that your lid will function correctly; if you cut straight down, the lid will fall into the pumpkin instead of resting on top. Once you have finished cutting, pry the top off and trim any hanging strings or seeds. Next, use the spoon to scoop out all of the seeds and place them in the bowl. Scrape the inside of the now-hollowed-out pumpkin of any loose strings. Pay special attention to the bottom. You want this to be as level as you can make it because this is where your candle is going to sit.

Using the template provided here, begin marking the pentacle design on the most favorable side on the pumpkin that will be the easiest to carve and will present the best.

If your pumpkin has a lot of flaws or blemishes, you can use the pattern to cut them out for a nicer finished look. Begin cutting along the lines, starting with the inverted pentagram on the center. Just as you created the lid, place the tip of the knife at the left edge of the dotted line with the sharp or serrated edge facing to the right. Push the knife slowly into the pumpkin and along the line.

When you have cut all five edges, you can push the pentagon out from the center. Next, cut out the triangle above the pentagon and push it out. Continue cutting out the triangles and last, cut out the pie shapes. If you make a mistake and cut all the way through one of the "arms" of the pentacle, you can salvage the design by rejoining the cut segments with toothpicks. If you go out of the lines, you can remove any remaining pen markings with a little rubbing alcohol.

Place the candle inside the pumpkin and light it with a long match or joss stick. Replace the lid, but if your pumpkin is on the small side, the inside of the top will scorch. You can leave the lid ajar, or just set it off to the side while the candle is burning. Your lantern is now ready for display, and it will surely frighten the unwelcome away.

Samhain Treat

Heat your oven to 350 degrees. Wash off your pumpkin seeds and dry them on paper towels. When dry, spread the seeds evenly in a single layer on an ungreased cookie sheet. Sprinkle them with salt, black pepper, and cayenne pepper. Bake for 15 minutes or until crisp and golden for a spicy Samhain treat!

THE DEAD SUPPER

One way to acknowledge an old custom is with a modern recipe.
Set out a "dead supper" for wandering spirits on Samhain night.
Discarnate spirits and the fallow earth are within the realms of
Hecate, the crone goddess of wisdom from the Greek pantheon.
Honor her at this time as well. You will need these things:

Two mixing bowls, one large and one small
Three knives, two dull and one sharp
A cookie sheet
A pastry brush, or a new and clean paintbrush suitable
    for using with food
1/3 cup butter
1¾ cups whole-wheat flour
3 tablespoons honey
2½ teaspoons baking powder
¼ teaspoon salt
⅛ teaspoon ground cloves
¾ teaspoon cinnamon
2 eggs
½ cup pomegranate seeds
4–6 tablespoons heavy cream
1 tablespoon water

1. Heat your oven to 400 degrees. In a small mixing bowl,
combine the cinnamon, clove, and salt. Stir in a clockwise
motion with the index finger of your left hand, saying:

"Lady of the crossroads three
With spices I come to honor thee
Cinnamon for the psychic eye
Clove to please you most
And salt to purify."

2. In the large bowl, combine the flour and baking powder. Add the spice mixture and the honey.

3. Using the two dull knives, cut in the butter using crossing motions until the mixture resembles fine crumbs. Stir in one beaten egg and the pomegranate seeds.

4. Sprinkle the mixture with a tablespoon of water, saying "By water, be thou blessed."

5. Add the cream very gradually, a tablespoonful at a time until the dough begins to leave the sides of the bowl.

6. Turn the dough out onto a lightly floured surface and knead about 10 times. Pat the dough into a rectangular shape about ½ inch thick, and using the sharp knife, cut the dough into small diamond shapes (about 15).

7. Place the cakes on an ungreased cookie sheet. Beat the other egg and, using the brush, paint the tops of the cakes

34

By Many Names

Samuin, Samain, Sauin, All Hallow's Eve, and Hallowe'en are some of the other names for Samhain. In the New World, Samhain was Christianized and became All Soul's Day or alternately, All Saint's Day. It is also celebrated as Dìa de los Muertos in lands that were conquered by the Spanish.

with egg. Bake the cakes for 10 to 15 minutes, or until they are golden brown.

8. Place the cakes along with a chalice or glass of dry red wine, or alternately, cranberry or pomegranate juice, on your doorstep next to your jack-o-lantern. Speak the following words aloud as you do so:

"Blessed spirits of my ancestors
And all my beloveds who have gone from this life,
Ye who dwell in the summerlands
Who hath crossed the long river of night
To realms beyond the veil
And sailed in the Makhent boat of Ra
In darkness to arrive on a distant shore
Far beyond my reach
Partake of this repast
I have set out for ye
And know that love yet flows in my blood
And the blood of the Mother flows in me."

If, in the morning, the cakes and wine are gone, you can take this to mean that spirits visited you in the night. If the cakes and wine remain at the light of day, pour the wine or juice as a libation into the earth and crumble and scatter the cakes to feed the birds.

Season Two

YULE

THE GOD IS REBORN

ON THE SHORTEST DAY of the year, the Earth is at its greatest distance from the sun on the celestial equator, and the sun shines directly over the Tropic of Capricorn. The winter solstice is the time of longest night, when the sun is at its lowest point on the horizon.

The word *solstice* comes from the Latin *sol stetit*, which literally means "sun stands still." Most likely, this description came from the illusion caused by the sun's position in the horizon. For six days around the time preceding and following the solstice, the sun appears to rise and set in the same place. The sleeping earth is filled with magic and mystery. We contemplate the beauty of the night sky and marvel at the rebirth of the light. Days that have grown increasingly shorter conclude with the celebration of Yule and the rebirth of the god.

The origins of Yule are speculative at best, with possible ties to the Saxon word for wheel, *hweol*. The "wheel" of the winter solstice could refer to the wheel of the year as well as the wheel that is the sun. The Yuletide celebration has its roots in the ancient Roman observance of Saturnalia, which was held from December 17 until December 25.

Saturnalia was the feast of the god Saturn, whose Grecian counterpart was Cronos. The rule of Saturn was said to be a Golden Age and is described by Ovid as a time of peace and bounty characterized by an absence of war and work. All beings lived beside one another in trust and perfect accord. There was no need to plow the land, for the land provided all manner of fruits and nuts and vegetation freely, without the toil of harvest. There were no city walls, for no one feared the threat of another. And there was but a single season, and that was lovely springtime when gentle fragrant breezes blew across the land.

Saturn is eventually overthrown by Jupiter, as Cronos is by Zeus. The Age of Gold comes to an end. The Age of Silver begins and with it, the cycle of changing seasons and the need for farming and protection from the elements.

THE WINTER SOLSTICE

Along with Samhain, the winter solstice and the observance of Yule are probably the most widely celebrated today of the ancient rituals. Although today Yule is linked to the Christian observance of the Nativity, there is no biblical or historical evidence that Christ was born on Christmas. Rather, December

25 was long held to be the celebration day of the Roman deity, Mithras. It is believed that the cult of Sol Invictus, or "invincible sun," with which Mithras is often associated, may have even predated the Romans by several hundred years. The Etruscans were known sun-worshippers and are largely associated with the beginnings of classical culture.

Regardless of its modern associations, it is no wonder that this time of year is and was celebrated as a holiday season. In addition to the advent of lengthening days, winter solstice was the time when much of the work of the year was complete. Harvest was long past. Provisions were stockpiled, and the ale was brewed. Winter solstice was unique in that it was a rare time for fresh meat. In pre-Christian times, the cycle of the seasons meant that fresh vegetables were available throughout the summer, but the long cold nights of winter made it the only time of year when the flesh of slaughtered animals would keep for any length of time without salting. So the winter solstice became characterized primarily by leisure and feasting.

The Roman Saturnalia was a carnival in the truest sense, its participants partaking in carnal as well as carnivorous pleasures. The drinking of alcoholic beverages factored heavily into Saturnalia celebrations, to the point where the holiday became synonymous with debauchery and lewd behavior. The Saturnalia festival included societal role reversal, where the masters would wait on their servants, who were accorded the very best that the house could afford. This can be interpreted as a mundane allegory to the divine exchange of power between the gods; the master becomes the servant as one age comes to an

39

end and another begins. Often, masters would use Saturnalia as an opportunity to make up for harsher treatment that occurred earlier in the year.

The celebration of the return of the light is also a metaphor for conception. The seed of the sleeping god is nestled within the womb of the goddess where it flourishes just as surely as the days begin to lengthen.

Legends and Lore: God of Light, God of Truth

The worship of the god Mithras is thought to have arrived in Rome from its Persian origins. Mithras is portrayed as a god of light and truth who reluctantly slaughters the sacred bull at the insistence of the sun god. As the magnificent beast lies dying, time comes into existence and the universe is created. The heavens above become the cloak of Mithras, emblazoned with the stars and studded with the planets. From the body of the bull the living earth arises; all plants, flowering and fruitful, along with creatures of the land and of the air spring forth. The elements and the seasons are created.

The blood of the bull pours forth, bestowing blessings upon the newly created land. The forces of evil respond by attempting to assert their dominance. They do not want the earth to be blessed or sacred and seek to impose their malevolent ways, preventing the blood sacrifice from protecting the land. Thus begins the struggle between good and evil, which will continue for all of time.

Celestial Events
THE HUNTER, THE BULL, AND
THE SEVEN SISTERS

When you gaze heavenward upon the winter sky, you may be struck by the fact that the stars seem so much brighter than usual. This is no illusion. The stars of the winter sky appear brighter because they in fact are! Almost half of the most luminous stars in the sky are visible during the long winter nights. Two of the most prominent winter constellations that lie closest to the zenith at this time of year are Orion and Taurus, and within Taurus is the bright star cluster the Pleiades.

The Culmination of Orion

Perhaps the most spectacular of all celestial displays is the constellation of Orion, the great hunter of Greek mythology. Of the twenty-five brightest stars, three of them (Betelgeuse, Bellatrix, and Rigel) are in Orion. In winter, Orion is truly one of the most dramatic of the constellations, even more so because it can be seen and enjoyed from all over the world. This is because the celestial equator passes very near to the northernmost star in Orion's belt.

If you bundle up and venture out at night around 10:30 and face the south, you can follow the horizon line upwards to the zenith, the point directly overhead. There, you will easily find Orion's belt, characterized by three bright laterally oriented stars.

Follow your eye westward to the upper left of the belt and you will see Betelgeuse, the orange-and-red-colored star. Next

41

to Betelgeuse toward the east and to the right is Bellatrix. To the lower left of the belt is Rigel, a bluish white star, and to the left of Rigel is Saiph. To the right of Bellatrix, you may be able to make out a faint string of stars that make up Orion's shield, raised perhaps to ward off the charge of Taurus, the celestial bull who approaches from the north.

Dangling from Orion's belt, you may see his sword, comprised of three faint stars in a vertical succession. Look closely at the center star. You will notice that it differs from the others in that its glow seems misty and strange. This is because it is not really a star at all. What you are actually seeing, and a good pair of binoculars will confirm this, is the Orion Nebula: a cosmic nursery where emerging stars are forming within clouds of dust and gas some 1,600 light years away.

This light that has traveled for 1,600 years to meet your eyes signifies the birth of new stars as well as the formation of their accompanying planets amidst the turbulence of stellar winds. As you celebrate the birth of the god and the return of the light, take some time to enjoy the wonder of the winter sky as you witness the birth of stars in the glow of their light.

In mythology, Orion was the greatest of hunters and boasted that he could kill any animal on Earth. Alas, he forgot about the scorpion, which wrought his demise at the bidding of the goddess Artemis. It is said that when Artemis killed Orion, she also killed his dog.

In the sky as well as in the myth, Sirius is the faithful companion to Orion and can be seen south of Orion's belt. Sirius, also known as the Dog Star, is the brightest star in the sky. Its name means "sparkling" or "scorching" in Greek. Sirius was called Sothis by the Egyptians, and the appearance of Sothis in the dawn sky predicted the flooding of the Nile, upon which Egypt's economy depended.

In mythology, Orion is characterized as a son of the immortal gods. Just as the reasons surrounding his death are highly speculative, so too is the circumstance of his origin. His parentage has been attributed to Poseidon, Zeus, and Hermes in different tellings of the story. Little is known about his mother.

Orion falls in love with the princess Merope, the daughter of Oenopion, king of the island of Chios. He hunts and kills all of the wild beasts of the island to win the favor of the king and, thus, Merope's hand in marriage. Oenopion is against the marriage, and rightfully so. During his courtship, Orion makes the strange choice of raping Merope. In revenge, Oenopion blinds Orion. His sight is later restored by the healing rays of the rising sun on the island of Lemnos. It is interesting to note that the myth surrounding one of the brightest constellations visible during the long night of the winter solstice alludes to the regenerative powers of the sun.

43

Taurus, the Celestial Bull

Orion raises his stellar shield as if he were fending off an attack from the charge of Taurus. Train your eyes to follow an imaginary line to the upper right of Orion's shield and you will find the characteristic triangle that comprises the face of the bull. Easy to recognize is Aldebaran, a bright orange star that makes up one tip of this V-shaped cluster of stars known as the

Hyades. The Hyades were the daughters of Atlas, and half sisters to the Pleiades. The horns of Taurus stretch out to the left.

The origins of the celestial bull lie in a tale of seduction and abduction. Although Taurus does not have a specific mythology, the constellation is most often associated with the story of Zeus and Europa.

When Zeus came to seduce Europa, the Phoenician princess, he took the form of a snow-white bull. Zeus spied the princess gathering flowers from a meadow by the sea and approached her as the handsome bull. Unable to resist its beauty, Europa caressed and kissed him. She climbed onto the bull's back and was carried away across the ocean all the way to Crete. Upon arriving in Crete, Zeus revealed his identity to Europa and won her over. The myth of the abduction of Europa has historical significance in that it establishes the etymology of the continent of Europe. Furthermore, the myth connects the bull to Crete, setting the stage for the Minotaur.

The Seven Sisters

In Greek mythology, the Pleiades are known as the Seven Sisters. The daughters of Atlas and Hesperis, their names are Electra, Maia, Taygete, Alcyone, Merope, Celaeno, and Sterope. Orion pursued them relentlessly, but he could never catch any of them. Zeus at last took pity on them and gave them a refuge in the starry sky. In the winter sky, it appears that Orion still persists in his pursuit, remaining unsuccessful, as the Pleiades are forever beyond his reach, lying to the northeast in the constellation Taurus. Six of the stars are readily visible to the unaided eye. The seventh is said to be visible only to those who possess "the sight."

The Pleiades are a distinctive and delightful cluster of stars. They have inspired folklore worldwide. Indigenous cultures across the globe have regarded the Pleiades as inspiration and omen: a harbinger of creation, an adornment of deity, and a herald of the apocalypse.

When you gaze upon the Pleiades, meditate on coven craft and the concepts of sisterhood. Even if your practice is solitary, you know in your heart that you are a part of a much larger circle. You can be assured that on the winter solstice, circles are being held across the world to honor the return of the sun god and to rekindle the solar flame.

By practicing Wicca, you are aligning yourself with the energies of the planet to bring about a much-needed balance to the world. Take a moment to appreciate the companionship of those with whom you share ritual. Think about your greatest teachers, your peers, and the ones that you will guide. Attune with witches across the globe as you envision circles of light

Mother to the God

Above the horns of the constellation Taurus, you will find Auriga, the charioteer. Auriga's most conspicuous star, Capella, lies just east of the zenith on the winter solstice. The ancient Greeks associated Capella with Amalthea, the she-goat and foster mother to Zeus. Many believe Amalthea represents an aspect of Capricorn.

soaring heavenward from cones of power raised throughout the longest night.

Astrological Influences
THE REIGN OF SAGITTARIUS AND CAPRICORN: HONOR AND WISDOM

The winter solstice sun is in Sagittarius, but this was not always the case. Hipparchus of Rhodes first revealed the slow and imperceptible movement of the stars, basing his findings on ancient Babylonian astronomical observations and star catalogs from around 1600 B.C. By comparing these records against his own observations (from 160 to 127 B.C.) he discovered the precession of equinoxes, the slow and subtle shift of the stars over several millennia.

Thousands of years ago, the winter solstice was in Capricorn. Today, on the day of the winter solstice, the sun shines directly over the Tropic of Capricorn, an imaginary line on the surface of the Earth, 23.5 degrees south of the equator. Because the exact time of the solstice varies from year to year, and the fact that in tropical astrology the winter solstice occurs on the "cusp," or turning point, in between Sagittarius and Capricorn, both astrological influences have significant relevance at this time.

Sagittarius and the Age of Honor
Sagittarius is ruled by the planet Jupiter, and it is Jupiter who overthrows Saturn in Roman mythology to bring about the

46

end of the Golden Age (and the basic underlying theme for the Saturnalia festival). The ninth sign of the zodiac, Sagittarius is a mutable fire sign and denotes positive, masculine energy. Due to its placement in the zodiac, some believe that when a soul incarnates in Sagittarius, it has moved through enough of the previous, "younger" signs to be in a place of honor and accomplishment.

Symbolized by the centaur and archer, Sagittarius is derived from the Latin word for arrow, *sagitta*. Arrows of inspiration illuminate the power and influence of Sagittarius, a sign associated with daring, enthusiasm, and philosophical thought. The centaur is a poignant symbol, an amalgamation of human and equine characteristics that represent the juxtaposition of primordial instinct and refined intellect. The human/animal combination can be seen as the struggle between order and chaos; base animal impulse and higher evolution; or the civilized world of man encroaching upon the uncontrollable world of nature.

In mythology, centaurs are described mainly in terms of this underlying conflict. They are often at the same time brutal and wise. One of the most famous centaurs, Chiron, was a tutor to some of the most notable heroes of Greek mythology, Hercules, Achilles, Jason, and Aesculapius among them. The son of Cronos and Philyra, Chiron was himself an immortal and the most refined centaur, an expert in ethics, music, medicine, as well as hunting and martial arts. He was accidentally shot by Hercules with a poisoned arrow, and, unable to heal himself, seemed to be fated to eternal suffering. Out of pity, Zeus released him from his immortality and honored him by turning him into the constellation Sagittarius.

47

The freedom from restraint, the wild and reckless abandon that accompanied Saturnalia and other winter solstice
observances is tempered by the appreciation of wisdom that the
centaur also represents. The centaur, however, is not the only
mythological blended creature that deserves contemplation at
this time of year.

Capricorn and the Age of Wisdom

There was a belief held through the Middle Ages that when
the sun shone directly over the Tropic of Capricorn, a gateway
opened between heaven and earth. This gateway was the portal
through which migrating souls would pass, some on their way
to earthly incarnation, others to eternal paradise. Additionally,
it was believed that gods would become mortals by traveling the
pathway of the sun from the sky to the Tropic of Capricorn.

The symbology of the astrological Capricorn is unique
and complicated. The tenth sign of the zodiac, Capricornus is
depicted as a fantastic creature with a goat for the upper half of
its body and the tail of a fish for the lower half. Capricornus is
truly a creature for all terrains. The goat half can be viewed as
the indomitable spirit capable of climbing mountains and faring
well on ground other beings would find too difficult. The fish
half denotes a being that can go with the flow, at home in the
water just as much as on land.

Capricornus has some confusing associations and has
been identified with several different mythological figures.
Many texts claim Capricornus is a representation of Aegipan,
the son resulting from the coupling of Zeus with the nymph Aex.

Other accounts claim Zeus lay with Boetis, a goat, who then bore Aegipan. Aegipan is identified by the Greeks as a form of the horned god Pan.

Whatever his matrilineal heritage, Aegipan was immortalized by Zeus for helping the god to recover his stolen sinews, which were severed and hidden by Typhon. Assisted by the god Hermes, Aegipan recovered Zeus's sinews from within the monster Delphyne and then changed himself into a sea-goat in order to escape. As a reward for his heroics, Zeus turned him into the constellation Capricornus.

Another interesting association of Capricornus is that of the foster mother to Zeus. When the ruler of the gods was but an infant, he was suckled by a goat. Some accounts say the goat belonged to the nymph Amalthea, while others claim that Amalthea was in fact herself the goat. It is said that out of gratitude, Zeus broke off the horn of the goat and presented it to Amalthea as an offering. She would never hunger nor thirst, and the horn would yield anything she wished for.

In this telling of the myth, we discover the origin of the fabled "horn of plenty": the bounty of the earth as expressed through the symbolism of the cornucopia. The river god Achelous ultimately

49

The Lords of Light

Some of the many names for the solar deity include Apollo (Greek), Belenus (Celtic), Llew Llaw Gyffes (British), Lugh Lamh-fada (Gaelic), Mithras (Roman), Osiris (Egyptian), and Ra (Egyptian).

inherited the magic horn. He incorporated it into his physicality, healing his own broken horn and thus becoming himself an amalgamation of goat and sea creature, or the icon of Capricornus.

The sun enters Capricorn on December 22. Ruled by the planet Saturn, Capricorn represents the tranquil state of existence of the retiring soul, one whose spiritual journey is approaching its end. Capricorn is characterized by a reliance on instinct and the observance of natural law. The wisdom of Capricorn is knowing when to pull back, to relax into the earth and integrate its stability into the magic of daily life.

Meditation
OF STARS AND SNOW

There is a Scottish Gaelic word that describes the depths of winter: *an dubhach,* "the gloom." However, the majesty of winter can be considered far from gloomy. There is a time for activity, and there is a time for quietness. On the winter solstice, contemplate the beneficence of stillness and solitude. The work of the harvest is over. The change from fall to winter is apparent, and energy is conserved for days of growth yet to come. Observe the silent earth, the sleeping seed, and marvel at the lengthening of days. Use this meditation to put you in tune to the energies of the season: the need for reflection, and the power of awakening.

● The longest night has arrived. The sky, once filled with migrating birds, is now empty. Trees have long since shed their

leaves, and their barren branches scratch their unique and tangled silhouettes against the sky. Hibernating animals settle down
inside their cozy dwellings, ready for the long sleep of winter.

● Around you there is silence. Stillness. You are lying
quietly on your back within a circle of tall stones. You gaze up
toward the sky, taking in the sharp chill of the winter air with
every breath. Around you, the frozen earth is lying in wait as
energy is conserved in preparation for the arrival of future
growth. Now is not the time for flourishing. Now is the time for
rest, and you relax totally, unaffected by the surrounding cold.

● As you exhale, you watch as your breath dissipates from
your body as though it were a cloud, rapidly disintegrating against
the night air. And with each breath, your spirit feels uplifted.
You feel your ethereal energy rising with each inhalation. As
you breath out, you rise a little higher. Each time you complete
the cycle of breath, your feelings of peace are augmented.

● Soon you feel as though you are floating high above the
Earth, your spirit buoyed by the surrounding serenity. All is still.
All is quiet. You are alone and experiencing a profound tranquil-
ity. You feel as though you have weightlessly risen above all
earthly cares and are now coming face to face with the mysteries of the cosmos.

● You gaze into the depths of space. The goddess Nuit
stretches her body across the vast sky. Her inky darkness contains the celestial sphere. All of the constellations of the zodiac
drift by, one by one. You feel as though time is suspended.

● You drift quietly as comets soar by, leaving blazing tracers of disintegrating ice in their wake. You are able to gaze across

the central plane of our Milky Way galaxy and witness the birth of new stars. Light is traveling all around you in a silent and radiant display. The coldness touches every particle of your being.

● You are one with this sensation of unity with the heavens, the stillness allowing you to direct your attention to otherwise unimaginable wonders. The darkness feels unending. Stars play with the particles in the atmosphere and reflect glittering brilliance.

● Beneath you lies the sleeping Earth. From your lofty vantage point, all is quiet. You float among the billowing clouds, breathing in the heavy moisture, and it becomes an integral part of you. The water that comprises the vast majority of your body is the very same water that gathers in the atmosphere high above the frozen Earth where the rivers and lakes lie motionless and covered with ice.

● With every breath, you feel as if you are dissolving into space and becoming a part of the moisture in the air. You are becoming one with the clouds, gently moving along the path of the north winds that blow, sending you slowly sailing through the sky. And the cold that grips your body is slowly transforming you.

● Planets drift silently by and you feel yourself gradually begin to change. You can no longer see the Earth, and you are enveloped in the cold softness of the gathering snow clouds. Tiny white crystals begin to form all around you, on you, and in you. They dance upon your skin and seem to permeate your being.

● Your blood and your tears are both part of a flowing crystal river filled with the magic of these tiny six-pointed stars. The sacred number of the goddess twice over! You marvel as the transformation continues. You feel as though your very breath is about to stop, but this causes you no distress.

● You feel the crystal energy forming inside you, touching and transforming your organs. Even your bones become crystals and as you stretch your arms and legs outward, you can feel your appendages also being incorporated into an outward manifestation of this inner structure that is taking shape.

● You are integrating with the snow crystals that are forming in the sky. You are the embodiment of purity. You float effortlessly and joyfully, a tiny mirror to the splendor of the scintillating stars. And then the most amazing thing happens.

● The Earth continues her heavenly rotation as you turn to face the sun. The light returns in a brilliant blaze erupting low on the eastern horizon. The light of the stars is no match for the glory of the returning light of the sun. One by one, they blink out their lights in deference to the power of the sun as it rises above the horizon. And you have finally reached the turning point of lengthening days.

● The sun radiates through the pure whiteness of your crystalline body. The light penetrates all of your pores, moving through you with radiant energy. As the white light moves through you, you separate it into all the colors of the spectrum. Acting as a prism, you change the light into its brilliant hues, releasing them throughout the sky.

● Regal purple, deep indigo, brilliant blue, tender green, warm yellow, burning orange, and fiery red pour through you, emblazoning the surrounding air with a rainbow of perfection.

You feel as if all of the highest possibilities that exist on Earth are within your grasp. Attainment of your potential seems imminent.

● The inspiring light of the sun begins to warm you, just enough that you begin to separate from your cloudlike crystal palace. You begin to drift independently, slowly spiraling downwards to the waiting Earth below.

● The sky begins to retreat from view as you gently fall through thick billowing cumulonimbus clouds, heavy with snow. The wind catches you and you dance on the breeze, floating off to the side and then back again in a slow but deliberate descent.

● The tops of the trees come into view, stark limbs bereft of leaves, glistening with dripping icicles frosted by the breath of winter. Down, down you glide, finally coming to rest on an undisturbed bank of snow.

● You meld with millions of other beings so very similar to yourself, but each entirely distinct. Even while you integrate with the world around you, you retain your unique individuality.

● You are experiencing divine unity as you rest with the sleeping Earth on the dawn of the shortest day. Oneness and originality coexist in a state of blessed peacefulness. This is the sun's gift to you; the knowledge that all you will ever need, you already possess. And you are the only one who can fulfill your unique mission in this life.

● The light of the sun reflects brilliantly against the whiteness of the surrounding snow. The brightness is almost overwhelming. You return to your body with the realization that you are an integral part of the divine matrix. And that actualizing your utmost potential is entirely up to you.

Ritual
CREATING THE YULE LOG

The tradition of harvesting, decorating, and burning the Yule log originated in pagan Scandinavia. The Yule log is the symbolic representation of the god of nature and vegetation. He is the Green Man who is cut down at the harvest season, only to be reborn and live again. The Yule log is lit; its flames invoke the rays of the sun, lighting the way for its triumphant return. The blaze of the Yule log dispels the darkness of winter, and its ashes are used to fertilize the earth. It is tradition to keep a portion of the Yule log with which to kindle the fire on the following year.

The Yule log can be any type of wood, but in the past it was usually a stout piece of oak or oak root, a thick branch from a fruit tree, or a birch log. The use of oak was to honor the rebirth of the Oak King, while the log of the fruit tree symbolized fertility. Birch was used most probably because its white bark was a reflection of the surrounding snow.

The procurement of the Yule log was done with great ceremony, and its presentation into the home can be a ritual of great significance today. The procession of the Yule log was said to generate good luck in the coming year. The more elaborate the ceremony, the better fortune with which the house would be blessed. We warm our hearts and our hearths as we enact the time-honored tradition of calling back the sun.

How you procure your Yule log will depend on where you live. If you are in the country with a proliferation of wooded areas, you may seek out an appropriate specimen, preferably dead on the ground. If you are taking from a living tree, do so with humility and clear intention. Ask for the tree's permission before you start cutting and leave a symbolic offering (such as a special crystal or other stone, or an herbal charm) in its place. You will need to select your Yule log well before the winter solstice because it will need some time to dry in order for it to burn properly.

If you are in the city, and there is no chance of harvesting or reclaiming a fallen log, you can visit your local Christmas tree lot. Most likely, you will be able to take home a discarded log free of charge. However you obtain your log, once it is in your home, treat it with respect as you would a ritual tool. It is a sacred symbol and will be a prominent feature in your winter solstice ritual.

Turn the log over and run your hands along it. Get to know the feel of the bark. Think about all the seasons it has endured, from sapling to tree, before ultimately coming to you. Trace your fingers along the rings on the cross sections. Repeating concentric circles are a reminder of the cyclical nature of life. Feel the residual energy of the elements: the wind that shook the

Yule Charm

To attune with the return of the sun, combine equal parts of bay laurel, cinnamon, and nutmeg in your mortar and pestle. Grind them together and place on a circle of green cloth. Bind it with red thread and carry it with you on the winter solstice. All three herbs are considered to be ruled by the sun. This charm will enhance psychic awareness, project positive energy, and emanate a warm and spicy aroma.

branches, the sun from which it photosynthesized its food, the water that nourished it and gave it life, and the dark earth that was home to its roots. Roll the log to see if it has a flat spot. If it is stable on its own, you may not need to reinforce it. If it rolls and rolls without ever finding a natural stopping place, you will need to make some minor modifications in order to stabilize it. You may take two small pieces of wood and nail them to the bottom.

Measure the length of the log. Using a hammer and a nail, lightly tap out eight equidistant starter holes. The nail should not penetrate the log very deeply, just enough so that the hole is visible and the nail is easy to remove. Now select a drill bit that will be approximately the same size as the diameter of the candles you plan to use, and drill the log in each of the eight holes to a depth of one inch. Place tapered candles in the holes.

Decorate the Yule log with cuttings of evergreen boughs or holly and ivy. You can even make a wreath of greens and place it on your altar (the Yule log would sit on top of the wreath). Evergreen is symbolic of hope. Even in the depths of winter, the flourishing green is a reminder of the eternal cycle of creation. Your Yule log is now ready for ceremony. On the day of the winter solstice, prepare your space for ritual. Do a purification ritual for your temple, your altar, and yourself. Cast the circle and call the quarters with this charge:

"Guardians of the east, we greet the dawn of the shortest day. All beginnings are contained within you. We beckon you to join us in our celebration of the returning light. May the spirits of air bless us with the winds of winter. Hail and welcome!

"Guardians of the south, we honor the return of your radiant light. The lengthening of days is upon us. Fly into our temple with your blessing and your grace. May the spirits of fire bless our home and hearth. Hail and welcome!

"Guardians of the west, the sun retreats to you and brings us to the longest night. Land of the dying sun, may he die no more, but be reborn anew. You spirits of water, who take many forms, bless us with your purity and grace. Hail and welcome!

"Guardians of the north, yours is the place of all endings. Our earthly path is guided by your Navigator's Star. In the depths of midnight, we dance upon the sleeping earth and ask for your blessing tonight. Hail and welcome!"

At this point in the ritual, the deities may be invoked. Choose a mother goddess archetype and a sun god to focus on as you symbolically rekindle the solar flame. Allow the room to be as dark as possible. This is the long dark of night, the very edge of transformation when life on earth begins to change yet again. Meditate in silence for a while and take in the surrounding darkness. When you are ready, celebrate the return of the sun by striking a match and lighting the first candle. If you are practicing alone, light the candles on the Yule log one by one, speaking each request as you go. If you practice with a coven, let each practitioner light a candle until all are illuminated. Say the following:

1. "The womb of the great mother is the cauldron of transformation. The spark contained within her signifies the rebirth of the god. May we receive her gift of the promise of new life."

2. "The darkness of the night sky is the body of the goddess. She is adorned with the beauty of the stars. May we radiate her sacred beauty in our works!"

3. "The energy of the sun is the essence of the god. Without him, life cannot be sustained. May we illuminate the path for his triumphant return."

4. "The fire of the hearth is symbolic of the warmth of the heart and the comfort of the home. May this temple be a home to the goddess and the god that all who enter here may receive their blessing."

5. "The spark of inspiration is the goddess's gift to the poet, the artist, the inventor, the creator. May she inspire us to do good works in the world for the benefit of all beings."

6. "Fire is a catalyst for transformation. May the goddess guide us as we seek to discard the unwanted burdens of life in order to make way for abundance."

7. "The body of the Green Man fertilizes the earth. From his ashes, new life is nourished. May he rise again to fulfill his promise to the earth."

8. "The light is a gift of clarity. May we discern the reality and the will of the universe, fulfilling our sacred purpose."

Partake of a feast either alone or with your companions as you watch the candles burn down. If you do not have a working fireplace, make sure you have a candle snuff close at hand so you can extinguish the candles when they start to burn low. To symbolize the returning light of the sun, you can surround the Yule log with candles in glass containers and let those candles burn

59

down completely. If you do have a hearth, you can pour a libation of wine over the Yule log and then set it on the fire to burn. Do not let it burn completely, but save a piece of it with which to kindle next year's fire. Gather the ashes and spread them upon the earth, or deposit them in your houseplants as the case may be.

If you do not have a hearth, extinguish the candles before they burn the surface of the log. You can save the whole log to reuse year after year. Share gifts with your companions, or write down your wishes for the coming year. These will be your gift to yourself. The solar flame has been rekindled. Release the directions, open the circle, and bask in the return of the light.

Practical Craft
HAND-POURED TAPER CANDLES

Many celebrations that occur on or around the winter solstice use candles as prominent symbols. The candle represents the warmth of the hearth, which is so important at this time of year. Candles have also been characterized as supporters of the sun,

By Many Names

The celebrations surrounding the winter solstice are also known as Yule, Midwinter, and Modranacht, or "Mother Night." On December 25, the Romans celebrated Sol Invictus (invincible sun). Sol Invictus became the state religion of Rome in A.D. 274.

tiny companions giving their strength to augment the powers of the sun god who is at his weakest at this point in time. Additionally, candles can be seen as a reflection of the beauty and wonder of the winter sky, filled with "night candles" in the form of its scintillating stars.

Tapered candles, called *cerei* by the Romans, were traditional gifts exchanged during the Saturnalia and symbolized the eternal flame. Creating your own candles is a lovely way to add special magic to your winter solstice observances. The following instructions will guide you in the creation of beautiful, slender tapers, quite suitable for adorning a Yule log. You can make these candles quite easily in your own kitchen without any specialized tools, mainly just household items, many of which you may already possess. You will need these things:

A pound or so of beeswax
Cotton string
A double boiler, which will be henceforth dedicated to candle-making only (after this exercise, it will be unsuitable for other uses such as cooking)
Small washers or nuts (the kind found in a hardware store, not a grocery store)
A ladle, also dedicated for candle-making henceforth
A dry cleaner's hanger (wire hanger with a cardboard dowel)
Sharp scissors or sharp knife

1. Cut four pieces of cotton string into 2-foot lengths. These will be the wicks of four pairs of beeswax tapers.

2. Tie a washer or nut onto the bottom of both ends of each string. These will serve as weights so your candles will be straight. Hang the weighted strings over the dry cleaner's hanger. You can place the hanger through the handle of a kitchen cabinet, or some other location that is close by but far away enough from the stove that your candles will be able to dry and not melt.

3. Fill the bottom chamber of the double boiler with water and set it to boil on medium heat on the stove. If you do not have a double boiler, you can improvise one using a medium saucepan for the lower chamber and a clean coffee can for the wax-melting chamber.

4. When the water starts to boil, place the beeswax in the upper chamber and set it on top of the boiling water. Allow the wax to melt. Lower the temperature of the flame just enough to keep the wax in a liquid state.

5. Take one weighted string off of the hanger and hold it high over the molten wax. You can hold your index and middle finger together and drape the middle of the string over your fingers to keep the wicks separated.

6. Scoop up a ladle full of hot wax and pour it down the string, starting from about four inches from the top. The wax will cool as it travels down the wick. Excess wax will drip back into the pot. Repeat this with the other half of the string. While you pour the first coat on the second wick, the first one will be drying. Continue pouring wax down each wick, alternating as you go. Allow some time in between pouring for the previous layer to dry, otherwise the application of the molten wax will melt the layer already applied to the wick and the process will take much longer. The wax will eventually begin to build up thickness. When the base of the candle is about a quarter of an inch thick (about the width of a pencil), place the pair back on the hanger to dry thoroughly. Repeat this process with the other wicks and you will have four pairs of beautiful beeswax tapers.

If you wish, you can create thicker candles by repeating the process and building up more and more layers of wax. (To make sure you don't run out of beeswax, try making fewer candles if you want them to be thicker.)

The candles are dry when the wax is no longer pliable and is cool to the touch. Using the scissors or sharp knife, remove the bottom end of the candle that contains the weight (washer or nut) and discard it. Trim the wicks to about a quarter of an inch, and your candles are ready to use.

Season Three

IMBOLC

FIRST LIGHT IN THE DARK OF WINTER

THE FIRST STIRRINGS OF NEW LIFE are felt as the great wheel turns from winter to spring. Water begins to move beneath the ice. We notice the lengthening of days. Dreams conceived on the winter solstice begin to take root. Although the weather is still wintry, there is no turning back on the journey to the sun's return. Winter's darkness begins to loosen its grip, and new beginnings are seen all around as spring approaches. This is a time for rebirth and healing, sacred to Brighid, goddess of poetry and arcane learning.

Brighid is unique among the Celtic pantheon. While the majority of Celtic deities were associated with features of the land and were usually confined to a specific geographical area, the worship of Brighid was, in contrast, very widespread. Her name comes from the Celtic root *Brig*, meaning "exalted." Considered to be a bringer of civilization, she is called the High One of Strength, daughter of the Dagda. The Dagda was the Celtic god of fertility and supreme deity of the land.

Brighid was the mother of Ruadán, half giant and half god. Early myths avow her a consort, the prominent Irish king, Bres Mac Elatha. Bres was appointed king by the Tuatha Dé Danaan and married to Brighid in a politic attempt to forge an alliance with Fomorian sea-giants. The worship of Brighid originated in the southeast region of Ireland known as Leinster and was attended by an all-female priesthood. She is often characterized as having two sisters, or alternately, a triple aspect whose attributes also include healing and smithcraft.

Many sources purport that Brighid the goddess was assimilated into St. Brigit of Christian lore. Certainly there are striking similarities between the goddess and the saint. The shrine of St. Brigit in Kildare is attended by nineteen nuns, echoing the exclusively female priesthood of the goddess Brighid. Additionally, many of the stories surrounding St. Brigit prove somewhat impossible for a single mortal woman to accomplish. Her legend claims she was born at sunrise and was so chaste a woman that she gouged out her own eyes in protest of her impending marriage and became a nun instead.

Other accounts claim she was a friend to the Virgin Mary, and in fact was Mary's midwife when the baby Jesus was born. She has also been described as Jesus' foster mother, and it is said she assisted Mary in her search for her son when he was lost in the temple and was later found instructing the rabbis. It does not take a huge leap of the intellect to discern the improbability that a blind nun from Ireland was able to escape the confines of time, let alone the limits of transportation, to be present in Bethlehem for the Nativity. The lines between the goddess and the saint are blurred, and Imbolc is celebrated as Candlemas, or the Candle Mass in honor of St. Brigit to this day.

IMBOLC

The Festival of Imbolc commences on February eve, or January 31, and usually concludes on February 2. Imbolc has three major associations: the veneration of fire and water, the quickening of new life in the womb, and the lactation of ewes. The association of Imbolc with fire comes from its place as the midpoint between the winter solstice and the vernal equinox. Celtic in origin, this sabbat hallows the midpoint of the changing season, rather than the day of change. Referred to as "the first light," the observance of Imbolc was marked by the traditional lighting of candles, signifying purification, inspiration, and growing light. Fire is also representative of the goddess Brighid in her aspect of patroness of smithcraft. In the fires of the forge, physical transformations occur. These changes are metaphoric, to symbolize the strengthening of the soul.

Another symbol of Brighid is the well. On Imbolc, processions were made to her sacred wells, which were typically adorned with greenery at this time, signifying the imminent return of spring. Devotees would circle the well deosil, or sunwise, before drinking of the waters in order to bring about good fortune. The procession was never made widdershins, or coun- terclockwise, as this was believed to bring ill luck. Water has long been associated with the power to heal, so it is no coinci- dence that Brighid, in her aspect as healer, would be associated with wells.

Another translation of Imbolc is "in the belly," referring to intrauterine fetal movement, also known as quickening. Imbolc is characterized by the preparation for birth. Brighid is a god- dess also associated with cattle, and the quickening of Imbolc often refers to the livestock that will be born in the spring. With its theme of preparation for birth, it is appropriate that Imbolc has evolved into an auspicious day for rituals of rebirth as well.

Traditionally at this time, the initiation of the witch is enacted. It is a time for reflecting on the nature of initiation and the evolution of the magical path. Like the dark reflections off the water of the surface of the well, the energy of Imbolc implores us to look deeper and contemplate the associations of water: mental acuity, emotional stability, and psychic ability. These may also be seen as manifestations of the gifts of Brighid, as sharpening of the mind is akin to the creative energy of Brighid as metalsmith. As a poet, Brighid balances the soul with inspi- ration and wisdom. The healing waters of her sacred well invite her devotee to scry and develop their psychic gifts.

The festival of Imbolc is alternately known as Oímelg, or "ewe's milk." The presence of lactating ewes was of great impor- tance at this time of year; it often meant the difference between life and death to the early Celts. Ewes only lactate when there are lambs to nurse, and in the intensity of February's cold, lactating ewes meant the presence of milk, cheese, and butter. While Imbolc is hailed as the beginning of spring, the weather bears a far greater resemblance to the grip of winter. If the stockpiled provisions of the Samhain harvest were not sufficient to last through the entire winter, ewe's milk (and its accompanying dairy derivatives) was the most immediate source of fresh food and a vital element to sustaining human life. In Ireland, the Imbolc feast was often celebrated with lamb's meat.

On February 2, the secular world acknowledges Groundhog Day, when the arrival of spring is determined by the presence or lack of the groundhog's shadow. Weather divination was common to Imbolc, and the weather of early February was long held to be a harbinger of spring. On Imbolc, the crone Cailleach's grip of winter begins to loosen. She goes forth in search of kindling so that she may keep her fires burning and extend the winter a little longer. If Imbolc is rainy and cloudy, she will

Legends and Lore: The Nine Gifts of Brighid

It was once believed that the druidic bards spoke a magickal language entirely their own and that they could only be understood by one another. In The Colloquy of the Two Sages, the mystical ancestry of Nede Mac Adne is revealed, and through him, the nine gifts of Brighid are named. Her gifts are described as spiritual appearances and blessings, enumerated as poetry, reflection, meditation, lore, research, great knowledge, intelligence, comprehension, and wisdom.

find nothing but damp twigs unsuitable for burning and will be unable to prolong the winter. If the day is dry and kindling is abundant, she will have plenty of fuel to feed her fire and prolong the cold of winter. Spring will be very far way. This is the probable origin of the fabled groundhog's shadow and its effect on the coming of spring—a modern weather divination that echoes Celtic folk beliefs of the past.

Imbolc celebrations were inextricably linked to the worship of Brighid. The lighting of candles was customary, signifying the growing strength of the sun and the lengthening of the days. The various regions of Ireland had equally various traditions of observance. Work was usually halted, and farmers would plow a symbolic furrow or plunge a ceremonial spade into the earth in an invocation of a bountiful harvest.

To access the power of Brighid the healer, people would leave ribbons or strips of cloth outdoors to catch the early morning dew and the first light of dawn. These ribbons were referred to as a *Brat Bríde*, meaning Brighid's cloak, and were placed on the body to cure ailments. Front doors were often left open to entice Brighid to enter. Often, ashes from the fire were gathered and spread upon the doorstep on February eve. In the morning, if any footprints appeared in the ashes, this was taken to mean that Brighid had indeed visited and was considered a promise of good fortune.

Celestial Events
THE LION AND THE TWINS

The night sky at this time of year displays two constellations with special significance to Imbolc: Leo and Gemini.

Leo, the Bringer of Spring

Although the constellation Leo will not culminate until April, the majestic lion of the starry night makes its first appearance above the horizon in early February. Rising in the east, the celestial lion has long been regarded as a herald of the coming spring. By 10:00 P.M. on February 1, calendrical Imbolc, the celestial lion will be above the eastern horizon.

Thought to be the first constellation to be identified pictorially, this grouping of stars has been associated with a lion since the earliest historical times, by the Babylonians, Egyptians, and Greeks alike. Leo's most prominent feature is the "sickle" of Leo, the pattern of stars that extends from its brightest star, Regulus. Regulus is a bluish star and burns hotter than the sun. *Regulus* is Latin for "prince" or "little king," further cementing the celestial lion's association with royalty. Algeiba is the companion of Regulus, and delineates the lion's mane. Marking the lion's tail is Denebola, while Coxa and Zosma indicate its hips and haunches.

In Greek mythology, the Nemean lion was an unconquerable beast that terrorized the people. The first labor of Hercules was to kill this lion, whose skin was reputed to be impenetrable by any weapon. Hercules overcame the lion by strangling it to death, and he wore its pelt thereafter as a symbol of his accomplishment. The star name *Zosma* means "girdle" or "loin-cloth." While it is extremely difficult to imagine a lion wearing such a costume, this may be a reference to the hide worn by Hercules invoking wildness and strength.

The lion is also a symbol of kingship. It is possible that the human head and lion's body of the Sphinx linked the power of the Egyptian kings to the symbol of Leo. The lion also appears in many versions of the tarot on the card representing strength. In the Rider-Waite deck, as well as its numerous derivatives, "Strength" is depicted as a serene-looking woman cradling the head of a lion. It hardly seems coincidental that one of the meanings of *Brighid* is also "strength."

The Twin Stars of Gemini

High overhead on February eve, the Gemini twins appear slightly to the southeast of the zenith point. Distinguished by the two bright stars Castor and Pollux, constellation Gemini is a highlight of the February sky. Pollux is the brighter of the two stars, while Castor lies nearest to Polaris, the pole star. In Greek and Roman mythology, Castor and Pollux are regarded as gods, spending half of their time on earth and the other half in heaven. They are the sons of Leda and the brothers of Helen of Troy. Their association with protection pertains mainly to ships at sea, connecting them to the water element, the veneration of which is prevalent at Imbolc. Water is also often used as an allegory for the emotions, which can be as tumultuous as a stormy sea. You can use the stars above as inspiration for invoking divine protection when delving into sensitive matters of the heart.

Astrological Influences
THE REIGN OF AQUARIUS AND THE AGE OF THE CRONE

How appropriate that on the commemoration of Brighid, tropical astrology brings the influence of the sun's power through the constellation known as the Water Bearer. The growing light of the sun corresponds with Brighid's fire aspect, while the water bearer evokes her sacred wells.

The eleventh zodiacal sign, Aquarius is a fixed air sign ruled by Uranus, representing the culmination of the soul's evolution. Themes of air and water are prevalent as the Aquarian age is characterized by spiritual vision, originality, individuality, and immortality. In arcane astrological calculations, the sun remained in Aquarius from January 21 until February 19. The sun in Aquarius meant the beginning of the spring rains. When Aquarius rises with the sun, winter has finally passed.

Today in astronomy, the sun is in Capricorn on Imbolc. As Capricorn is a blended creature with marine attributes, the zodiacal association of Imbolc with water still stands. Both Capricorn and Aquarius have been interpreted as references to the coming of the seasonal rains.

Aquarius radiates tolerance, acceptance, and wisdom as suggested by its connection to the crone. In Egyptian mythology, Aquarius is represented by Hapi, God of the Nile. As water bearer, Hapi holds two overflowing vessels symbolizing the Nile of the North and the Nile of the South. In the sign of Aquarius, the soul begins the preparations for the end of its journey and

73

ultimately for rebirth, one of the major themes associated with Imbolc.

The mythological figure most closely associated with Aquarius is the Trojan prince, Ganymede. A youth of incomparable beauty, Ganymede attracted the affection of Zeus. Taking on the form of a majestic eagle, Zeus absconded with the youth and brought him to Mount Olympus to serve as his erotic partner as well as the nectar-bearer to the gods.

Ganymede was the son of Tros, the grandson of Dardanos, who was a son of Zeus and founder of the first settlement of Troy. To compensate the family for their grief at the loss of their son, Zeus gave Tros a gift of horses and comforted him with the knowledge that his son would enjoy eternal youth, beauty, and immortality.

In Grecian art, Ganymede is most often depicted with a look of sensual abandon and trust as he is carried away by the great eagle. He has come to represent the model of the often same-sex relationships between gods and mortals of Greek mythology. However, the astrological sign of Aquarius does not imply any proclivity toward homosexuality as its associated myth might suggest.

74

Meditation
DELVING INTO THE DEPTHS
OF THE WELL

Our link to the goddess becomes clearer as we are reminded of our sacred origin. From the mysterious depths of the womb, the quickening of new life is felt. Use this meditation to attune with the healing powers of water and its biological significance.

● A cobblestone path leads you up a gently sloping hill. The air is crisp and chilly. There are no clouds in the sky and the sun shines brightly. Even on a day as clear as this, the warmth of the sun is barely a match for the brisk February air.

● You are carrying a candle, and its light dances as the wind teases the fire. You cup the flame with your hand to protect it from the playful breeze. It gives you some precious warmth on this bright and cold day.

● You reach the top of the hill and your path ends. The stones that you followed convene in an elaborate spiral mosaic at the center of which lies the object of your destination, the sacred well of Brighid.

● The well is closed and you walk up to it, setting your candle down beside you. You look at the heavy lid, a thick and sturdy circular slab of wood adorned in metal with the *vesica piscis,* a sacred symbol of the goddess: two circles joined in graceful harmony.

● You trace the intertwined circles with your fingers, running your hand along the cold iron. You can see ancient hammer marks from when the cover was forged centuries ago. The circles remind you of the cycle of creation. The sun. The moon. Infinity.

● You slide open the latch and with all your strength, you pull the great cover open. You are amazed to find a great proliferation of plant life pouring forth! Dense ferns and duckweed, nourished by the fresh waters, thrive and flourish.

You kneel down and gaze at your own reflection among the plants. You peer at the image of your face; the reflection is dark and your features are barely discernible. You lean in closer. Your breath moves across the water's surface, creating gentle ripples. Your reflection oscillates in response.

You lean closer still, touching your lips to the water's surface. It is surprisingly warm! In fact, the water seems to be the same temperature as that of your body. You lean in farther, submerging your face. You exhale slowly, delighting as the bubbles move across your cheeks and through your hair.

You submerge your entire head. You forget to breath. You don't need to. A great power is pulling you in. You do not lose your balance, but very slowly and deliberately, you slide headfirst into the inviting waters. The water permeates your body. Waves of pleasure and peace surround you. You drink in serenity and feel as if your soul is being restored. Invigorated, you somersault through the water and gaze upward. You see the light of the sun glimmering through the particles suspended in the water.

You stroke the smooth stones that mark the sides of the well. It seems as if there is life in every tiny crevice. Aquiferous plants outline the stones with gentle shades of green. You turn upside down, wanting to explore deeper.

You have become a water spirit, moving effortlessly down through the deep spring. Light begins to leave you as you descend. You move faster and faster, traveling headfirst into the unknown, your body undulating as you go.

You begin to feel the pull of a strong current, pulling you down, down, down. Even if you wanted to turn back now, you could not. The surface is far behind you and there is now a rushing sound in your ears. It grows louder and louder when suddenly you find yourself at the mouth of a great underground river. This is the source of the spring that feeds the well. It is easily ten times as wide.

● You move through the river and discover that many paths diverge from this point. You are at the point where three rivers meet. Far beneath the earth, vast networks of water flow with great force bringing precious nutrients to surrounding earth.

● You are a passenger on the mighty currents of the well's best-kept secret. The force of these swiftly moving waters is incredible. They sweep you along, the strength of the current moving you and moving through you.

● The water permeates every pore of your body, healing all that it touches. With every hydrating caress, you are restored. Age and weariness turns to youth and vitality. Cuts and scrapes are mended. Internal organs are replenished. Scars disappear. Anything at all that has ever been wrong with you is now righted. Wounds of the past are healed. Emotional pain is replaced by a sense of oneness with all beings, peace, and serenity. Physical discomfort and pain diminishes to the point where it ceases to exist.

77

● You feel only relaxation and invigoration. Cells regenerate, your mind clears, and your body strengthens. You are perfect, whole and intact.

● Suddenly, you are in charge of your soul's journey once again. No longer swept along, your movement is now deliberate. You travel great distances underground, hurtling and swimming through the darkness with joy.

● Eventually, you begin to see light again. The mouth of the river gapes and you tumble head over heels into the ocean. You float to the surface, the sudden salinity effortlessly bearing you up. The sun touches your face. You open your mouth and gulp great gasps of fresh ocean air.

● You are carried by the waves to a sandy shore. Gently, the waves deposit you on the pristine beach, lapping over you and then retreating to the sea. You feel totally renewed, cleansed by the freshness of the spring and purified by the salt of the sea.

● You have been to the meeting of the waters and experienced the deep mysteries that lie far beneath the surface of the earth. You marvel at your journey, feeling for the first time that you have an awareness and sense of your own conception, that of traveling through a long tube in darkness to a vast and watery womb to be reborn anew as a perfect being.

● You are reminded of the interconnectedness of all things, how the forces of nature mirror the functions of the human form, and know that beneath your feet, the awesome healing power of the goddess courses through the earth. And that this awesome healing power also flows through you.

Elixir of Brighid

Warm a pint of milk in a small saucepan. Add a teaspoon of honey and ⅛ teaspoon of vanilla. Stir constantly until the honey is dissolved. Allow the mixture to cool to room temperature. Pour it into your chalice and drink to taste the sweetness of the goddess.

Ritual

THROUGH THE GODDESS,
WE ARE REBORN

With its theme of preparation for birth, Imbolc is an ideal time to honor those who have deepened their practice by enacting initiation rites. It may also serve as a time for the rededication of one's self to the craft for those who have already attained initiation. An initiation rite celebrates the rebirth of the soul through the path of the goddess; it also acknowledges those who have attained a certain level of proficiency and experience in the craft.

Most initiations are done within the context of a coven with the priestess and/or priest conducting the ritual for the benefit of the candidate. The priestess does not actually confer the initiation; that is done by the deities invoked. The priestess serves as the conduit through which the rite is administered and the channel through which the will of the deities may be ascertained. No one person can tell the true moment of a spiritual awakening. An initiation may be a celebration of a psychic evolution that has already occurred. Here you will find an eclectic initiatory rite based on Western occult ritual structure that would be suitable for an Imbolc celebration.

Begin by purifying the circle and all present with sage and a salt-and-water asperge. The priestess casts the circle while the initiate awaits outside the circle. She may say:

"Daughter of sunrise who paints the morning sky with her brilliant light, descend into this temple to witness the rebirth of the

spirit. *By the air that is her breath, I invoke the spirits of the east. Hail and welcome!*

"The fires of the spirit burn bright as we celebrate the return of the light. Fires of the forge that transform the soul, strengthen us as we seek to know your mystery. By the flames that illuminate the cauldron, I invoke the spirits of the south. Hail and welcome!

"Deep waters of the sacred well, we call upon you to cleanse and restore us. Healer of all wounds, come to us now and lend us your aid. By the water that is her blood, I invoke the west. Hail and welcome!

"Dark earth, keeper of all of life's secrets, most powerful ancient mother of creation, come into this temple to witness our sacred rite. It is you whom we seek to honor, to tread gently upon, to greet in wholeness at the end of our span. By the earth that is her body, I invoke the north. Hail and welcome!

"Hear the words of the great goddess, midwife of souls, she who holds the flame of inspiration in her hand."

At this point, the priestess may channel an oracle or use a variation of what follows, derived from the *Colloquy of the Two Sages*, an Irish mythological text dating from the twelfth century:

"At the moment of your birth I stood watching, waiting to greet you, loving you even as your mother cried out. A spark of the divine forever lives in you. This was my gift to you, your birthright, which you nurtured. As it grew, so too grew your sacred gifts. You learned to trust your intuition and have followed the spiral path back to me. I call you forth now to be known again as my child. For I am

the mother of poetry; my voice cries out in joy through the heart that sings. I am the mother of reflection; I maintain the order of the universe and set the balance of the spinning earth. I am the mother of meditation. I give the soul respite and preserve the peace of the planet. I am the mother of lore; I promote the cause of the just and see that their legends are preserved. I am the mother of research; through me all requests are granted. I am the mother of great knowledge; I reward the eager mind with inspiration. I am the giver of all gifts and I receive the souls of my devotees at the end of their life's journey. I am the mother of intelligence; I bring order to chaos and reveal the truth to the prepared. I am the mother of understanding; I nourish my children and care for them utterly. I am the mother of wisdom, the exalted one of strength. In me, all rivers converge, and all fires burn. The stars swirl around me in their eternal dance. My children all are blessed."

It is customary for an initiate to have a spiritual guide to assist them in the preparation for initiation. Usually, this is the person who introduced the individual to the coven. The spirit guide waits outside the circle with the candidate for initiation. After the oracle, the spirit guide knocks on the door.

PRIESTESS: "Who seeks entrance into this holy temple of the goddess?"

SPIRIT GUIDE: "One who seeks to dedicate herself to the inner mysteries. She is called _____ [the candidate provides her magickal name]."

Using her athalme, the priestess cuts the spirit guide into the circle. The candidate stands before her, blindfolded or veiled. The priestess holds her athalme before the candidate and advises her:

"You are about to enter into a vortex of power, to step between the worlds where birth and death, light and dark, become one. From a woman you were born into this world, and by women you are born into this circle. Are you willing to press on in the face of your fear?"

THE CANDIDATE REPLIES: "I am."

PRIESTESS: "So mote it be. Enter into the circle in perfect love and perfect trust." The priestess takes a long red cord from the altar and loosely winds it around the candidate's wrists, saying:

"You enter into this circle by your own free will to dedicate yourself to the goddess. You are not bound, neither are you free."

The candidate is admitted to the circle and stands in the center, representing the infant soul in the womb. A cone of power is raised around her using this chant:

"By her breath and by her broom
The light returns, the light returns!
By her word and in her womb
The light returns, the light returns!
The fire burns, the wheel turns,
The light returns, the light returns!
A tiny spark dispels the dark,
The light returns, the light returns!"

When the energy reaches its peak, the priestess joins the candidate in the center of the circle. She removes the candidate's blindfold and the chanting stops.

82

PRIESTESS: "Which goddess do you choose, that you may honor her always and follow in her path?"

CANDIDATE: "I choose the goddess Brighid [or substitute the name of the chosen deity]."

The priestess unbinds the cord from the candidate's wrist and takes her measure from crown to toe. She cuts the cord, ties a knot at each end, and drapes it around the candidate's shoulders.

PRIESTESS, CALLING THE CANDIDATE BY HER CHOSEN MAGICKAL NAME: "_____, daughter of Brighid, accept this symbol of your connection to the divine mother. All beginnings and all endings; all that is contained herein now belongs to the goddess.

"What offerings do you bring to this temple, to honor your chosen goddess?"

CANDIDATE: "I bring this incense to inspire us and to honor Brighid in her aspect of poet. I bring this candle to evoke the transformational flame of her forge. I bring these flowers as evidence of the life-giving powers of her sacred water."

PRIESTESS: "I accept these gifts as an offering to Brighid. May you be blessed with her powers of healing, inspiration, and craft." The priestess anoints the brow of the candidate with water from the altar. She turns the candidate around to face the coven and asks: "Who among you will stand with this candidate to accept her initiation?"

The spirit guide comes forward and replies, "In the name of Brighid [or her own chosen goddess], I accept this initiation."

She may even give a description of the qualities that the candidate possesses that make her worthy of initiation. These may include her dedication to the coven, rituals attended or enacted,

83

and insights gained, as well as any spiritual or psychic talents she may possess. Other coven members may accept the initiation as well.

PRIESTESS: "_____, you have been accepted before this company and the presence of all. As a child of the goddess, you may perform a self-blessing to dedicate yourself to your newly chosen path."

The candidate may use the following blessing, derived from the Five-Fold Kiss by Gerald Gardner. She may alternately compose an original self-blessing in advance to be used here.

"Blessed be my feet, that have brought me to this path.
May I ever walk in wisdom and radiate the love of the goddess.
Blessed be my knees that kneel before the sacred altar.
May I show forth both honor and humility.
Blessed be my womb, that brings forth new life.
May I be a channel for the power of the goddess.
Blessed be my breasts, formed in beauty and in strength.
May I love and know love.
Blessed be my lips, that speak her sacred name.
May I manifest divine truth in my work."

PRIESTESS: "May you go forth and radiate the power of the goddess in your works, that your deeds may harm none, but be of benefit to all beings. So mote it be."

ALL REPLY: "So mote it be!"

The priestess may raise a chalice to give thanks to the deities present at the ritual. The chalice may be passed around the circle, as each coven member welcomes the new initiate as a peer, and recounts the stories of her own initiation. After the chalice has been passed, feasting and merriment may commence. The priestess will determine when it is time to open the circle and release the deities and the directions, so that all may go forth, grounded and with divine blessings.

DIVINATION AND MEDITATION

If your practice is solitary, or if you do not require initiatory rites, you may enact less ceremonial but no less meaningful observances of Imbolc. Following are some ritual suggestions that can be performed alone or with a coven.

Waters of the World

To attune with the energy of Imbolc and Brighid, you may perform a scrying ritual that symbolizes gazing into Brighid's well. Scrying is a divination technique used to open the psychic mind and eye so that visions may be granted and information ascertained. You will need a large bowl of dark-colored glass; cobalt or obsidian will work the best. You may also place a black mirror at the bottom of the bowl if you wish.

Take a moment to think about your surroundings and the nature of water. Think of all the forms in which water may manifest. Water comprises the oceans, rivers, lakes, streams, ponds, and puddles. Water evaporates and forms clouds. When the clouds get too heavy, they fall to earth as rain, sleet, snow, and ice. Water makes up 98 percent of the molecules of our bodies; it is in our blood, our tears, our sweat, our spit, and our secretions. Water cleanses and water purifies. Without it, we could live only a few days.

Think of all the places that water occurs around you and begin gathering water from as many different sources as you can. You will need at least three different sources, even if you are landlocked and all you can muster is faucet water, bottled spring water, and rain or a few drops from a really good cry. Be creative.

Place the vessels of water upon your altar among lighted candles. Prepare your scrying bowl; making sure the bowl is very clean and dry. Burn some incense and state your intention aloud before the altar. What is it that you are seeking? Perhaps it is a glimpse into the future, or some insight into a current situation that you are facing. Whatever it is, do not be afraid to name your desire. Recite this chant as you pour the waters into the bowl.

"Eye of Brighid,
Eye of the mind,
Mother blessed and divine,
Who dwells both in and out of time,
Into your darksome depths I scry.
In you all beginnings and endings lie.
Come to my aid and be my guide.
Assist me in what I hope to find.
What lies before me and behind?
This I charge thee with this rhyme:

Grant me what I know is mine!
For I am your anointed daughter
And the keeper of your sacred water."

Sit quietly and allow yourself to access your subconscious mind as you gaze into the bowl. It may seem as though the surface becomes cloudy at some point. This is an indication that you are scrying correctly, that the "mists" are gathering. Look deeper for patterns in the water that may symbolize an answer to your question. When you are satisfied, give thanks to the goddess for her assistance and pour the waters into the earth. Let your candles burn down in honor of the first light in winter's darkness.

Illuminating the Cauldron

Fill your cauldron with dark earth. Take nine tapered candles (like the ones used for the Yule log) and plant them into the earth in a spiral pattern beginning in the center and continuing deosil, or clockwise. With each candle, contemplate a different aspect of Imbolc.

87

1. Light the candle in the middle first, picturing the first light penetrating winter's darkness.

2. With the second candle, welcome the spring and picture the great wheel of the year turning to the halfway point. The cauldron is the womb of the goddess, the "belly" of Imbolc.

3. Think of the magic of the beginnings of life and all the possibility contained as new life emerges as you light the third candle. Each new dawn is a clean slate that may bring you closer to realizing your dreams.

4. With the fourth candle, imagine the circumstances surrounding your own physical birth. Picture your relationship to your biological mother as a reflection of your relationship to the divine mother. All of us need mothering in one form or another. By facing your own vulnerability, you are preparing yourself for rebirth.

5. As you light the fifth candle, focus on the lessons your spiritual path has taught you. There are intimate truths that you have undoubtedly discovered. Give thanks for challenges met and knowledge gained.

6. The sixth candle represents the unknown, the lessons that lie in front of you and all the things you have yet to learn. Cultivate humility even as you recount your accomplishments.

7. Light the seventh candle and meditate on all the things you wish to *change*. They can be material, physical, or spiritual. Use your magic to make a positive impact on your life.

8. The eighth candle represents the things you most need to heal. These include the physical ailments of yourself and of others, the suffering of the planet, rifts in relationships, and so on. Invoke healing into your life, and make room for it to begin. Release old wounds and past hurts. Take responsibility for your health in a new way. Focus on the best possible outcomes for situations that are beyond your control or influence.

9. As you light the ninth and final candle, welcome inspiration into your practice. Ask the goddess to illuminate her presence in a new way. Sing. Write a poem in her honor. Even if you are not particularly artistic, use the energy of the season to assist you in manifesting your magic in a tangible way. Create a special charm or a new blend of incense. Whatever your chosen method of expression, ask the goddess to inspire you and show forth her beauty in your work.

Practical Crafts
BRIGHID'S CROSS, THE EYE OF BRIGHID, AND THE BRIDE'S BED

As a goddess of many lands, Brighid's worship inspired many rituals involving the creation of crosses and images from reeds, cornhusks, rushes, straw, and other vegetation. Here are some traditional crafts that were created in her honor.

Crios Bridghe

Crios bridghe, or Brighid's cross, is a bit of a misnomer as this is a circular rather than a four-way motif as its name suggests. Originating in the western region of Connemara, the *crios bridghe* is made from lengths of rye straw traditionally cut by hand and braided into a rope. The rope is then formed into a circle. The circle is believed to be protective; those who jump through it are blessed with good health and good fortune. It is also symbolic of rebirth. You may construct one of your own by gathering up vines that grow locally. This can even be an ecological gesture of stewardship of the land if you choose to harvest vines that are dangerous to other plant life. Stranglevine in

89

the North and kudzu in the South are two examples of aggressive vines that have adverse effects on the surrounding trees. You can cut them down with your scythe, and in so doing, make a small improvement in the health of the host tree.

Cut three sections of vine about five feet long. Bind one end together with a white ribbon, symbolizing Brighid's purity. Braid them together by taking one of the outside vines and laying it over the middle vine, alternating as you go. When you get to the end, bind again with white ribbon. Bend the braid into a circle and tightly tie the ends of the ribbons together. Alternately, you can use raffia, which is available in most craft stores and would be suitable for all of these crafts.

Another version of Brighid's cross is a four-way motif that resembles a swastika, an ancient symbol that represents the sun. It is usually made from reeds and symbolizes an invitation to Brighid, invoking her presence in the home. In Kildare, Ireland, the cross was plaited from green straw. It was hung on the door for a year as a protective charm against fires. On the next Imbolc, when the cross had dried and turned from green to gold, it was stored in the rafters and replaced with a fresh green cross.

Brighid's Eye

The Eye of Brighid, also sometimes called the God's Eye, is made by taking two sticks of equal length and tying them together to make a cross. Reeds or ribbons are then looped around each arm of the cross in a clockwise fashion, creating a tight diamond-shaped pattern. The Eye of Brighid can also be woven with many colors of yarn or thread and then hung on the wall or door for a protective house-blessing.

The Bride's Bed

In Scotland, it was customary for young women to construct an image of Brighid out of rushes or reeds. The doll was then dressed with lace and ribbons, and a shell necklace tied around her "heart." This necklace was referred to as "the guiding star."

The doll was often carried from house to house. She was then put to bed in a ceremonial basket also decorated with ribbons and lace, accompanied by the soft singing of lullabies. The basket would often be lined with the residual rushes left over from the weaving of Brighid's cross. These rushes were never carelessly discarded, but carefully covered with a white cloth to make a bed for the goddess. It was believed that the effigy would come alive with the spirit of Brighid during the night.

By Many Names

Imbolg, Olmec, Oímelg, Candlemas, and Laa'l Breeshey are some of the other names for Imbolc.

Season Four

OSTARA
SPRING'S ARRIVAL

THE SUN CROSSES THE celestial equator heading north, bringing about a magical state of balance as equal day and equal night are manifested in perfect twelve-hour divisions. As it slowly journeys north along the ecliptic, the suns remains in the sky a little longer each night, setting exactly due west near the time of the vernal equinox, usually on or around March 20.

Ushering in the official first day of spring, the astronomical view of the equinox occurs when the sun is at the exact intersection of the celestial equator and the ecliptic. The vernal equinox marks the beginning of the tropical year. Originally established by Caesar and Sosigenes, the tropical year is 365.242 days long and is determined by the precise interval between two vernal equinoxes. The tropical year differs slightly from the sidereal year, which measures the revolution of the earth around the sun and lasts 365.256 days.

The second of the solar festivals in the Wiccan year, the arrival of spring is celebrated as the maiden goddess awakens from her long sleep of dreams. The newness of spring is observed in the tender green of the bough and the eminent potentiality of life's reawakening. The sky, no longer empty, resounds with the joyful song of birds. The equilibrium between polarities brings us awareness of the duality of nature; light balances the dark as life balances death. The snows of winter have melted, leaving the earth supple and moist. The branches of trees that stood stark and bare for so long are now covered with tight buds, soon to erupt in an explosion of color and scent. The world seems to awaken; newness, possibility, and purity are in the air.

There are few things more exciting than something that is on the verge of becoming. At this time, potential is everywhere. We bask in the miracle of the dawning springtime. In regions close to the Mediterranean, the summer crops have already begun sprouting up through the earth. In the north, the time for seeding is at hand. Newborn foals and calves struggle to their feet and begin to romp on shaky legs. The greening of the earth begins.

THE VERNAL EQUINOX

In the Wiccan year, the vernal equinox is celebrated as the return of the spring maiden from her winter sleep of death. She is called the Kore, and also Persephone. She is reunited with the Mother Goddess of the earth, signaling the renewal of life. The vernal equinox is also the time to revere the sacred marriage between the goddess and the god. The sun god born at the winter solstice grows into the vitality of youth and is seen as the perfect consort to the flowering maiden.

Ideal and innocent, this divine pair will consummate their love with the next turn of the wheel when the Beltane fires are lit on the eve of the first of May. Other mystery cycles in the Wiccan tradition of seasonal observances celebrate the hierogamy, or divine marriage, between the goddess and the god at springtime. Just as the earth is supple and moist and prime for planting, so too is the goddess thought of as ripe and ready to receive the seed of her lover, which will culminate with the birth of the god nine months later.

One of the most prominent symbols of the vernal equinox is the egg. To many cultures, the egg represents the cyclical rebirth of nature. It is frequently equated with the sun god, as suggested by the rich golden hue of the yolk. The egg is also considered a symbol of creation. Some genesis myths claim that the universe was created when a divine serpent wrapped itself around and cracked the cosmic egg. The upper half became the firmament and the lower fragment, the earth below. The egg retains symbolic aspects of both god and goddess; the appearance of solar affinity and the creative powers of birth. This indeed makes it a fitting emblem for the first day of equal light and dark. Additionally, eggs were a welcome dietary supplement to the meals of pre-Christian civilizations. Traditionally, the last of the winter stores were consumed as part of the spring celebrations, and people would hunt for and collect the many-colored eggs from the nests of wild birds. It has often been suggested that mankind developed the inspiration for basket-weaving by observing the nests of birds.

Celebrations of the vernal equinox are linked to many goddesses of fertility, predominantly the Saxon goddess Eostre and her Germanic counterpart, Ostara, who gives her name to the Wiccan sabbat. Eostre is associated with the dawn, rebirth, and the spring. She seems to possess a symbolic affinity with rabbits, as they factor into several of her myths. Some accounts claim that rabbits were considered sacred to Eostre, and that she

Legends and Lore: The Hare in the Moon

One popular telling of the myth of Eostre is that she possessed as a companion and familiar spirit a great bird whose wings were frozen. The frozen wings morphed into the ears of a rabbit, and the goddess's sacred totem is said to retain the characteristics of both animals. The rabbit is a fitting symbol of the springtime as it is a creature well known for its quick reproductive capabilities. The average gestational period for rabbits is one month, making them a natural emblem for fertility. Since there are no known Saxon deities depicted with a rabbit's head, as Eostre is often described, it is possible that the rabbit-like appearance attributed to Eostre comes from the illusion produced by craters on the moon. Goddesses have long been associated with the moon, and many agree that the lunar surface does indeed contain what appears to be the distinct form of a rabbit as seen from Earth.

herself was known to take on the form of a rabbit. Others call her Eostar and claim that rabbits were killed in sacrifice to her.

Ostara shares many similarities to Eostre, and not just in name. Ostara, too, is a goddess of spring. She is also called Ostare, goddess of the dawn. Her celebrations often occurred at sunrise on hilltops and centered on growth and the renewal of life. Prayers were made to assure the abundance of crops, and eggs were ritually eaten and exchanged as talismans in her honor. Eggs were also left on the graves of the beloved deceased, perhaps as a testament to the belief in reincarnation. Offering an egg to the dead was a way of calling for their rebirth and return.

The rites of spring were by no means exclusive to the Teutonic and Saxon people. In ancient Phrygia, the spring equinox was revered as the rebirth of Attis, lover and consort to Cybele, the supreme goddess of the land. Cybele was the embodiment of the fertile earth, and her celebrations have been described as orgiastic, characterized by singing, dancing, reveling, and even castration for the male followers. The resurrection of Attis was observed on March 25. In Mesopotamia, the restoration of Ishtar and Tammuz was celebrated in the spring, as was the union of Inanna and Dimuzi.

97

In Greece, the blooming of the red anemone flower was held to be the sign of the flowering of Adonis. Beloved of both Aphrodite and Persephone, Adonis was a handsome youth who met his tragic fate on the tusks of a wild boar that he had wounded in a hunt. Prior to his death, Zeus had intervened between the goddesses contesting for his affection and decreed that Adonis would spend half of the year with Aphrodite and the other half with Persephone, echoing the journey of Persephone herself and bringing balance to the masculine and feminine polarities of seasonal myth.

Celestial Events
THE BEAR, THE VIRGIN, AND THE HERDSMAN

While the stars of the spring sky are somewhat pale in comparison with their winter counterparts, the warmer temperatures of the dawning spring allow for more comfortable stargazing in the evenings. The sky on a clear spring night provides serene beauty with its wide variety of characters, boasting some of the largest constellations. Two of the three largest constellations to span the night sky are now visible.

Overhead, you will find many bright stars to serve as your guide to the celestial sphere, along with the circumpolar constellation known by many names: The Great Bear, the Big Dipper, the Wagon, and the Plow all refer to the constellation of Ursa Major. While it is easy to locate overhead in the spring, it never seems to completely disappear below the horizon. Virgo also dominates the night sky, along with Boötes the herdsman.

Ursa Major, the Great Bear
The mythological origins of the Great Bear, like many other constellations, begin with the amorous exploits of Zeus, king of Mount Olympus and father of the gods of the classical Greek

pantheon. Callisto was the daughter of Lycaon, a king of Arcadia. When Zeus spied her hunting along the train of Artemis in the mountains of Acadia, he fell in love with her and seduced her. She bore him a son, Arcas, who grew to be a great hunter like his mother.

Callisto was changed into a bear by one of the gods, although which one we cannot be certain. Some accounts attribute the transformation to Artemis, who was enraged by Callisto's transgression of the sacrifice of her chastity. Others claim that Zeus changed Callisto into a bear to protect her from the jealous wrath of his wife, Hera. Another telling of the myth states that Hera turned Callisto into a bear after the birth of Arcas.

When Arcas grew to manhood, Hera placed Callisto before him, hoping that the agile young hunter, ignorant that he was hunting his mother, would kill the bear. But Zeus became aware of the plot to kill Callisto and snatched her away, placing her safe from Hera's rage in the heavens above. Arcas was eventually placed by her side and became Ursa Minor, the lesser bear.

Furious that her rival would be accorded such an honor, Hera convinced the god of the sea never to permit Callisto and Arcas to enter his waters. Homer best describes this mythological explanation of the circumpolar nature of Ursa Major in the *Iliad*:

> *. . . and the Great Bear that mankind calls the Wagon:*
> *She on wheels on her axis always fixed,*
> *Watching the Hunter,*
> *And she alone is denied a plunge in the Ocean's baths.*

The bear is also closely associated with the lunar maiden goddess Artemis. Called "The Untamed One," Artemis is often represented by the great she-bear. Rites of passage for pubescent Grecian girls invoked Artemis in her aspect of bear. The young female participants enacted a dance in her honor, called the *arkteuein*, meaning, "acting the bear."

The girls were often sequestered and engaged in wild behaviors. Dressed in bearskins, they would abandon grooming, eat raw foods, and wrestle. Their isolation would last a week or more and concluded with the call to the dance. They would dance to near exhaustion, tearing off their bearskin cloaks in a dramatic allegory of shedding their animal nature, and complete the dance naked.

At about 10:30 on the night of the vernal equinox, Ursa Major can be clearly seen just north of the zenith. Its most recognizable feature is the "big dipper," which is in fact just an asterism of Ursa Major. Finding the big dipper is relatively easy, even from urban locations. Face the south and search for the outline of the dipper's familiar "bowl" and accompanying "handle." The bear's body is the bowl of the dipper and the handle is the bear's tail.

Beyond the stars Merak and Dubhe, to the right, is the snout of the bear, and beneath the "bowl" are its legs. Ursa Major serves as a wonderful guide to the other major constellations of the spring sky as well as the pointer to the pole star, Polaris. To locate Polaris, imagine a line extending from Merak through Dubhe, the two stars in the dipper's bowl that lie farthest away from the handle. This line will point directly to the North Star. Polaris, also called the North Star, is the center point around which the entire celestial sphere appears to revolve. It has been referred to as "the pillar of heaven" and marks the end of Ursa Minor.

When you gaze upon the Great Bear of the night sky, let her serve as a reminder of the awakening earth beneath your feet, for the Great Bear reaches her highest point as the sleeping bears on earth arise from months of hibernation. The slumbering creatures of the land come to life again, and the earth teems with vitality once more.

Virgo, Maiden of the Harvest

Second only to Hydra, the celestial water snake, Virgo is one of the largest constellations to span the night sky. The virgin goddess of the celestial sphere has been identified with the Saxon goddess Eostre. She has also often been interpreted to have associations with the harvest, as Spica, her brightest star, references a sheaf of wheat. Virgo is thought by many to be a representation of the goddess Demeter. However, Virgo's name would seem to suggest a correlation with Persephone, a maiden or "virgin" goddess, rather than a mother aspect (as represented by Demeter, mother of Persephone).

A different interpretation links Virgo with Hygeia, the daughter of the renowned physician Aesculapius. Described as unmarried, Hygeia is considered the patroness of women's health. A 1493 depiction of Virgo from *Abstrolabum Planus* shows

101

an angelic maiden as a winged creature holding the caduceus, a wand intertwined with two snakes, the emblem of the medical profession. Snakes are also regarded as a symbol of rebirth. Other accounts associate Virgo with the star maiden, Astraea. Astraea is a goddess of purity, hence her correlation with the celestial virgin. Astraea, however, is more correctly identified with Libra, which follows Virgo on the ecliptic.

You can locate Virgo in the night sky by drawing an imaginary arc from the handle of the big dipper that extends through Arcturus, the brightest star in the spring sky, all the way to Spica, the brightest star in Virgo. Picture Spica as a sheaf of wheat that the maiden goddess holds in her hand. As you gaze upon the starry spring maiden, may you be blessed with good health in many aspects: physical, emotional, and spiritual.

Boötes, the Plowman

The star Arcturus is the most prominent feature of Boötes. Without the distinction of containing the brightest star in the spring sky, the rest of the kite-shaped constellation would be otherwise difficult to locate. You will find Boötes to the east of Ursa Major and to the north of Virgo. While there is no specific mythology attached to Boötes, he has been called "the one who drives the plow," presumably due to his proximity to Ursa Major. His status as plowman to one of the most recognizable constellations makes him an appropriate companion to Virgo in her aspect as harvest goddess. As you begin planting the seeds of desire this spring, allow yourself to envision your harvest as the light of the stars shines down upon you.

Astrological Influences
THE REIGN OF PISCES AND ARIES;
DEATH AND REBIRTH

With new life emerging all around and light and dark in perfect balance, the spring equinox ushers in a changing of the ages. The end of Pisces and the beginning of Aries is symbolic of death and rebirth, for the zodiac itself ends with the sign Pisces and begins with the sign Aries. The spring equinox has a crucial role in determining what many astrologers consider to be the beginning and ending of astrological ages. The concept of an astrological age refers to the idea that certain astrological signs dominate certain historical periods. The sign of influence is commonly held to be the sign in which the spring equinox occurs. During the Hellenistic period, which lasted from approximately 300 to 50 B.C., the spring equinox was in Aries. Due to the phenomenon known as the precession of equinoxes, the spring equinox has been slowly traveling backwards through the zodiac over thousands and thousands of years. Each astrological "age" is thought to last approximately 2,150 years, although the actual date when one age begins and another ends is all but impossible to determine due to the distance between the zodiacal constellations.

The precession of equinoxes is the astronomical fact behind the metaphysical concept of the emerging Aquarian Age, or New Age as it is alternately known. In roughly another 600 years, the spring equinox will cross over from Pisces into Aquarius. When the reign of Pisces and the culture of death comes to an end, Aquarian virtues such as increased perception, wisdom, and tolerance will dominate the cultural landscape.

Pisces and the Age of Death

Positioned at the end of the zodiac, Pisces represents the place in a soul's evolution where it is believed to have incarnated through all of the preceding astrological signs and have attained significant cumulative experience so that it may finally be released from the cycle of life, death, and rebirth. Pisces is the greatest of all endings. Ruled by the planet Neptune, the glyph of Pisces is the trident of Poseidon. The trident has been identified by some as a symbol of the triple goddess, most likely because it is a three-way motif.

Represented by the fish, Pisces is a mutable water sign linked to the dream state of psychic and spiritual awareness. Pisces represents the journey's culmination. Its symbolic fish is at home exploring the darkest depths of consciousness and emotion where others would be overwhelmed. As the spring equinox is the time of balance of light and dark, Pisces represents the darkness just as it begins its retreat. It is a stark contrast to the ebullient energy of Aries.

Pisces is one of the few dual signs of the zodiac, in that its representation is depicted as two fish that are usually enjoined by a cord connecting their tails or alternately with their tails intertwined. The fish swim in opposite directions, calling to mind the symbolism of yin and yang: the balance of light and dark and of feminine and masculine energies. In mythology, the dual fish of Pisces have been described as a representation of

Aphrodite and Eros. The supreme goddess of love and her son transformed themselves into fish and jumped into the sea in order to avoid Typhon, a monstrous son of Gaia sent to destroy the Olympians.

As the fish is a creature that lives exclusively in the water, it can be said that the realm of Pisces is in fact another world, coexisting yet separate from the world we live in. In tropical astrology, the sun enters Pisces on February 20 and remains until March 20. In astronomy, the sun enters Pisces on March 12 and remains until April 19. Pisces lives where the zodiac ends, thriving in the mysterious waters that lie just beyond our reach.

Aries and the Age of Awareness

Astrologers regard the vernal equinox with great importance because it is considered to be the beginning of the zodiac. Referred to as "the first point of Aries," it sets the wheel of the celestial sphere in motion. Aries represents the awakening soul, full of impetuosity and the unconscious egocentrism possessed by children.

Aries is symbolized by the ram, and his glyph is the ram's head. This is often seen as a reference to being "headstrong," a characteristic that those born under this sign are reputed to possess. Aries marks the very beginning of the soul's journey, characterized by innocence and the dawning of awareness. Light begins to overtake the darkness at last and the cycle of life begins in earnest once more.

A cardinal fire sign ruled by Mars, Aries contains the most developed mythology of all of the zodiacal signs. Despite his reputation for an enormous amorous appetite (and a legion of mythological bastards to substantiate this claim), Zeus had but a single son that was born of his wife, Hera. And that was Aries, the god of war. Aries, or Mars, as the Romans called him, is characterized as an impulsive, fate-defying, insolent, and handsome youth. Although he never married, he has been linked to Aphrodite and was the father of Eros, the god of love. As Aphrodite and Eros are seen as the mythological inspiration for the sign of Pisces, the cycle of life and death comes full circle with the paternal role of Aries. He is also called the father of the Amazons, a race of powerful and dangerous female warriors purported to live among the Caucasus Mountains of southwestern Russia.

Meditation
THE AWAKENING EARTH AND SPRING'S RETURN

The maiden goddess arises as we focus on the return of Persephone from the land of the dead. Follow her sacred journey from springtime to springtime as you imagine yourself to be a part of the matrix of nature.

● Imagine that you are the beginnings of a flower. You are a tightly wrapped bud, your petals are closed, protected by a shield of green leaves, hugging you closely in a fierce embrace. The sun radiates its fiery brilliance and the days are growing longer and longer. You are bathed in light and caressed by gentle breezes. The rain falls softly upon you. You remain tight and closed as a fist, longing to stretch out as the days lengthen. The sun continues to shine and the nourishing rains continue to tenderly fall.

You feel yourself expanding from within, and you burst forth through the firm green leaves. Your colorful petals extend outward to greet the welcoming sun as it rises through the cool morning air. You stretch out and sigh, glistening with drops of dew. Light pours down upon you. You feel yourself swell and open even further, releasing an attractive fragrance and reveling in your loveliness. You are surrounded by luscious perfume. The enticing aroma wafts through the air and the attraction begins.

Insects fly to you, descending upon your velvety petals. They inhabit you, crawling upon you and within you. They are the catalyst for your complete transformation. You begin to swell and grow from the inside. Your petals begin to wither. One by one they fall away and drift to the ground below. You are swollen with liquid and a growing potential for total change.

You are transforming from flower to fruit and hang heavier and heavier on the vine. Winds blow and you slowly sway in the breeze. The sun streams down, but somehow less so. The nights are growing longer and your branch begins to weaken.

A sudden gust of wind overtakes you and suddenly you have broken free of the branch. You feel suspended in time, free falling and spinning in slow motion. Air passes over you as you move through it until you finally contact the soft earth waiting patiently below. You roll a small distance and then come to a complete stop. You lie there, motionless, slowly softening and fermenting.

● Your skin begins to loosen as your internal moisture is gradually absorbed by the earth upon which you rest. Little by little and day by day, you are increasingly becoming one with the earth. Every day you sink a little bit deeper into her soft and welcoming soil. Every passing day, you resemble your former self less and less. As time passes, you dissolve completely into the earth, sinking deep beneath the surface with every rainfall.

● Nights lengthen. The sun shines for you less and less. You are no longer large, soft, or ripe, but tiny and hard and sleeping within the sacred ground upon which you once lay.

● Snow begins to fall. At first it seems mild and soft, but as the long nights progress you find yourself increasingly buried deep within a winter blanket of shimmering frost. The long sleep has begun.

● You are unmoving and silent, fast asleep far beneath layers and layers of frozen ice. In complete darkness you lie, knowing that from full blossom to burgeoning fruit, your new incarnation is nothing less than sheer potential for new life, waiting to unfold. Time passes.

● Days begin to lengthen. The ice gradually begins to melt into small flowing rivulets. The streams run over you and through you. You are now saturated with water. It is all around you, permeating every part of your being.

● You begin to swell larger and larger until your cellulose sarcophagus can no longer contain you. You reach deep into the earth, sending a tiny new root downward, relishing the moisture and taking in rich nutrients from the soil. You pull them into yourself and start to send the energy upwards.

● You burst forth into the light of day in a shiny green shoot, relishing the light that you have not seen for so long. You stretch out and reach upwards to the streaming sun, uncurling perfect new baby green leaves.

● You take in the energy from the sun and transform it into growth. You reach higher and higher, simultaneously sending your roots deeper and deeper into the earth. You are connected to both the earth and the sky, the perfect balance of thriving life in between the worlds.

● Days begin to lengthen once again. You grow stronger and thicker. The wind that once wreaked havoc with your tender form now feels like a gentle caress against your strengthening trunk. You are ready to expand.

● You separate yourself into branches, sending out fresh green shoots in all directions, reaching ever skyward. Rain that once threatened to beat you down is now a delightful elixir, enabling you to continue your rapid growth.

● Your leaves are now a lush bounty, covering every branch and twig with shining green. You feel the wind in a thousand ways. Your complex root system knows the depths of the earth intimately. The sun is your best friend, enabling you to turn energy into life force.

● In addition to the abundance of leaves, you begin to form buds exactly like you once were. You explode in the full flora of spring, perfuming the air, enticing all things that fly to take refuge in your branches and blossoms. Not just a miracle of creation in your own right, you are now the shelter and support for other living creatures. Squirrels leap playfully from branch to bough, birds make their home in your limbs as you cradle and protect their woven nests. You are heavy with fruit that will all too soon fall to the ground with the promise of beginning the sacred cycle all over again.

● Nights begin to turn cold, and the bright daylight that gave you fortitude begins to slowly fade into twilight. The twilight lingers longer than before and seems to come on sooner. The wind against which you once held strong now begins to strip you of your leaves. The shining green gives way to a burst of fire as you turn to golden hues of amber and deep reds.

● The leaves spiral downward, buffeted by the wind as they make the journey to the ground below, covering the earth in a glorious mantle of autumn. You stand naked and alone against the coming cold, bracing yourself for the approaching storms.

● Your branches are now completely bare. The birds that once found refuge in your boughs have all left for warmer climes. In the enfolding darkness, you wait, warmed only by preciously short days when the sun tries to break through the consuming cold. You know that you have moved far from the sun, but you also hold the promise of the sun's return. Patiently, you wait.

● Your exposed branches are vulnerable to the frozen waters that once ran over you, now clinging to your limbs in crystalline icicles. You lie fallow and wait. Beneath the bare branches is green wood. You sleep in the mere illusion of death, life patiently waiting for the right time to emerge. You know that the earth is continuing her arduous journey around the sun, slowly bringing you back to the place and time of fruition. You have not moved, but you have changed in a thousand ways.

● The ice begins to melt. Sunlight keeps you company more and more. The seemingly unending darkness begins to recede. One day, a person approaches you. She bows before you in reverence, placing herbs and crystals at the base of your form.

● In one smooth motion, this person raises a small scythe over her head and cleanly cleaves one of your small lower branches from you in a smooth stroke. She pauses for a moment, singing a low chant, and bends to touch you and sit with you awhile. Instinctively, you know the purpose of this deed. The reverence with which the cut was made, the offering placed before you can only mean one thing; that this person has utmost respect for the thousands of changes you have endured. She understands the darkness and the light, the passage of time, the abundance and the emptiness, the cycle of life, death, and rebirth. By taking a small piece of you, she is taking a potent reminder of this entire spectrum of your existence.

● You stretch and smile. As the sun drops beneath the horizon and twilight descends, a witch goes home to build and consecrate a wand. Spring is coming. It is almost time to grow again.

III

Ritual
OSTARA INVOCATION FOR VITALITY

With its emphasis on new beginnings and new life, Ostara is an ideal time to call a renewed sense of energy to ourselves so that we may flourish along with the greening earth. Begin with an invigorating ritual bath. You may combine equal amounts of sea salt and Epsom salt in a bowl (about ⅛ cup of each) and add a handful of crushed peppermint leaves.

Pour the mixture into a muslin pouch or large tea bag and steep in a hot bath. Allow the salts to dissolve and the water to cool until it is comfortable. Immerse yourself in the bath with a soaked cloth draped over your face. Breathe in the stimulating essence of the herb as you allow the warm water to ease your muscles.

Use the cloth to exfoliate your body, envisioning the cold and stagnant energy being scrubbed away and replaced with an exciting new dawn. As you wash your face, think on these words:

"I cleanse myself in the blessed company of the tender green of the earth. May my thoughts and desires be aligned with the divine nature of the goddess. Allow my eyes to discern beauty wherever it lies. Let me breathe in the invigorating air. May it renew my blood with its purity. May my ears be filled with the happy songs of the birds of the sky. May my lips curl in a delightful smile at the new life unfolding around me. May my voice be clear and strong, raised in praise to the great lady of all beginnings. May my heart beat steady and sure, filled with love and not longing. May I never hunger nor thirst, but accept the abundance that is her gift to the land. May the powerful sinews of my arms stretch to the sky to invoke her grace. My hands will work the transformation of her lovely crafts. My legs will move in a joyful dance. My feet will walk gently upon the renewing earth, and the land shall become more beautiful because of my care."

After immersing yourself in water, it is now time to envision yourself aligning with the creatures of the land and of the air. Allow yourself to air-dry. As the water evaporates from your skin, think of the snakes that shed their skin in their cycle of renewal and the birds that molt, revealing new feathers, soft and crisp. Next, light a candle and place a plate of fresh sprouts before you. Hold the plate high above the candle, saying this:

"May the spark of life and the flame of vitality imbue these living seeds with power and strength. Goddess great, goddess green, blessings on these thriving seeds! As I consume them, hear my plea: Heal me. Grant me what I need."

As you chew the sprouts, envision yourself taking in the energy of the springtime. As you swallow, envision yourself taking the healing power of the goddess inside you, replenishing your internal organs, enlivening your body with healthful energy, with blessings inside and out.

Practical Craft
DECORATING EGGS FOR OSTARA

Although the egg appears in the symbolism of many cultures, some of the best examples of the ritual decoration of eggs come from Ukrainian folk art. Egg dyeing was a special ritual, passed down from mother to daughter for generations. The two main types of decoration are called *krashanka* and *pysanka*.

Krashanka, derived from the word *kraska,* meaning "color," refers to an egg dyed a single brilliant color. These eggs were usually eaten and were believed to possess talismanic powers. *Krashanky* (plural of *krashanka*) shells placed under haystacks or stashed within the thatched roof of peasants' homes were a protective charm against high winds. *Krashanky* were rolled in green oats and then buried to protect the harvest against destructive winds or excessive rain. *Krashanky* were also used for healing physical ailments as well as protecting the crops. An entire *krashanka* would be worn around the neck of the ill person, or the egg would be placed on the infected parts of the body as a cure.

Pysanky (plural of *pysanka*), which comes from the word *pysaty,* meaning "to write," involves intricate decoration using a variety of symbols and a wide array of colors. These eggs were not eaten, but rather displayed in the home, carried as talismans, and exchanged as gifts. *Pysanky* were believed to provide protection against fire and lightning. An old folk legend claimed that *pysanky* ruled the very fate of the world. Only *pysanky* could stem the flood of evil that threatened to encompass the world. If *pysanky* were numerous, then love would conquer evil. But if the custom were to fall away, a vicious monster would be unleashed and the world would be consumed.

Creating Krashanky

To create your own edible *krashanky,* start by hard-boiling some eggs. Bring 2 quarts of water to a rolling boil. Using a slotted spoon, place the eggs gently in the boiling water. Boil the eggs for approximately 12 to 15 minutes. Using the slotted spoon, remove them from the pot and transfer them into a bowl of cold water. Allow the eggs to cool and dry.

To make your own natural and nontoxic dyes, combine your dye material with a quart of boiling water. Strain the liquid into a jar and add 2 tablespoons of white vinegar to set the dye. Here are some suggestions for natural vegetable dye ingredients and the colors they will yield:

Natural Egg Dyes

Vegetation	Amount	Color
Red cabbage	4 cups, sliced or shredded	Light blue
Beets	4 cups, shredded	Light purple
Yellow onion	4 cups of skins only	Orange
Spinach	4 cups, chopped	Green

Once you have prepared the dyes, soak the eggs in the color of your choice, making sure that the liquid covers the eggs completely. The longer the eggs soak, the deeper the color will be; however, they will not be nearly as dark as the dye liquid itself. For the most intense color, allow the eggs to soak overnight in the refrigerator. You can use the egg carton to dry them in. Be careful when handling freshly dyed eggs, as some of the dye will rub off. When *krashanky* are eaten, it is considered bad luck to discard the shells carelessly. Burning the shells or casting them into flowing water are the acceptable methods of disposal.

115

Creating Pysanky

Since *pysanky* are not meant to be eaten, they can be decorated raw. If you want to keep them for a long period of time, you can blow out the contents of the egg after carefully piercing a small hole in either end. You can also boil them for an extended period of time (30 minutes or longer). This will render the eggs inedible and their contents will eventually dry.

Before dyeing your eggs, take a crayon or a piece of wax and inscribe your desired symbols and motifs on the surface of the dry egg. The traditional method of applying wax begins with making a special tool called a *kistky*. The *kistky* is basically a small metal cone with a tiny pinpoint opening tied or otherwise attached to a stick at a right angle. The *kistky* can be dipped into a pool of molten beeswax (such as the wax that accumulates around the wick of a burning candle) and the wax then applied to the surface of the egg. It helps if the egg itself is slightly warm so that the wax does not cool too quickly.

After applying an initial design, immerse the egg in the dye as directed for making *krashanky*, using the lightest desirable color first. The wax will form a barrier preventing the dye from adhering to the marked portions of the egg. The wax designs will be lighter and will stand out against the dyed background. This technique is similar to that used in the batik process.

Cover in wax any areas from the first dye bath that you want to leave undisturbed and dye the egg in progressively darker colors. You can also create concentric rings or bands around the eggs by placing rubber bands around the egg, both

By Many Names

Ostara, Lady Day, Alban Eiler, and the First Point of Aries are some of the names by which the vernal equinox is known.

vertically and horizontally. This method can assist you in blocking off fields for repeating design motifs. One of the challenges of decorating *pysanky* is the uneven and rounded surface of the eggs. By dividing the surface into sections, you will have greater success achieving a balanced and pleasing design.

When you are finished applying designs and are satisfied with the depth of colors, allow the egg to dry completely. You can then remove the wax by warming the egg in an oven for a few minutes, then wiping the wax off with a clean towel. The most common design motifs are geometric, animal, and plant motifs. Each pattern has its own special meaning.

Symbolic Patterns and Their Meanings

Motif	Pattern	Meaning
Geometric	Dots	The starry sky
Geometric	Parallel lines	Eternity
Geometric	Triangles	Triple goddess
Geometric	Star	The sun god
Geometric	Parallel broken lines	Death (rarely used)
Geometric	Spiral (single)	Eye
Plant	Eight-pointed star	Rose
Plant	Arrows	Pine tree/ youth and health
Plant	Spiral (series)	Apples
Plant	Tree	Life
Animal	Butterfly	Transformation
Animal	Spider	Fate
Animal	Bird	Fertility

Feel free to experiment. Some alternative ingredients for dyes that you may consider using are these:

- Pomegranate juice instead of water to achieve red tones
- Grape juice instead of water to achieve pink
- Strong coffee instead of water for beige and mocha
- Paprika mixed with water for orange

Recipe
SOLAR CROSS ABUNDANCE BUNS

One of the most satisfying magical endeavors is creating yeast-based breads. There are few other spells that provide such immediate gratification as well as physical and spiritual nourishment. By combining the four elements—air (in the bubbles produced by the activated yeast), fire (the temperature inside your oven), water (the liquid with which the dough is mixed), and earth (the flour)—you create an offering to the deities and healthful nutrition for your body. Transformation is rapid and tangible, a physical echo of a spiritual change that you can literally take in. You can begin this recipe on the night before the equinox and finish it in the morning.

These delicious fruit-filled buns have long been a traditional part of the springtime feast. Emblazoned with an equal-armed cross on the top, they symbolize the union of masculine and feminine energy. The cross represents the male principle and phallic symbol. The roundness of the bun is symbolic of

the goddess element, feminine and beautiful. Here is a simple
recipe to grace your table as you celebrate the dawning spring
with ritual feasting. You will need these things:

Parchment paper (for baking, usually found near the wax
    paper in the grocery store)
Quill and vegetable ink
A large cookie sheet, or multiple baking pans
A large bowl
A small saucepan
Plastic wrap
A clean kitchen towel
Bolline
A pastry brush
5 cups unbleached flour
5 eggs
1 cup milk
⅓ cup melted butter
2 tablespoons active dry yeast
½ cup sugar
2 teaspoons Celtic sea salt
1 teaspoon honey
1 teaspoon cinnamon
½ teaspoon nutmeg
⅓ cup dried cranberries
⅓ cup raisins
⅓ cup golden raisins
⅓ cup dried currants

1. In a small saucepan, warm the milk gently. The chill of refrigeration should be gone, but it should not be too hot to touch. Do *not* overheat or boil the milk. Add the teaspoon of honey, stirring constantly until it is dissolved. Remove from heat, and sprinkle the yeast into the warm milk and leave it alone while you assemble the other ingredients.

2. In a large bowl, combine the sugar, salt, cinnamon, and nutmeg and blend them together. Add the melted butter and four eggs. Pour in the milk and mix all ingredients together.

3. Begin adding the flour one cup at a time until incorporated, mixing vigorously until sticky and smooth. Cover the bowl with plastic wrap and allow the dough to rest for half an hour.

4. Begin kneading the dough, adding the dried fruit until it is well mixed. At this point, the dough will be very sticky. You will need to add additional flour, a little at a time before kneading by hand. Shape the dough into a ball and place it in a greased bowl.

5. Cover the bowl with plastic wrap, and let the dough rise overnight in the refrigerator.

6. Take the parchment paper and write upon it in pen and ink (*not* pencil) your hopes and dreams for the spring. The paper can be as large as your baking pan, if you wish, but write only on one side of the paper. Ask for blessings for yourself and for your beloveds. Write notes of praise to the goddess with whom you feel the closest affinity and ask that her abundance manifest in your life. Ask that this abundance be revealed to you in the manner in which it may be of the highest benefit to the world. Kiss the parchment and let it sit out on your table all night, preferably near a window if possible. Go to sleep and envision your fondest dreams coming true.

7. In the morning, take the dough out of the refrigerator and let it sit until it reaches room temperature (about half an hour). Take the parchment paper and place it written side facing down upon your cookie sheets or baking pans.

8. Turn the dough onto a lightly floured surface and divide it into thirds, then divide each third in half, and then half again, and so forth until you have 24 pieces. Form them into little round balls and place them ½ inch apart on top of the parchment. Cover them with the kitchen towel and set them to rise in a warm sunny spot until they have doubled in size (about 1½ hours).

9. Preheat your oven to 400 degrees. When the buns have doubled, carefully slash them across the top with the bolline, marking each one with a cross. Think of the light overtaking the darkness as you mark the solar cross on each one.

10. Separate one egg and discard the yolk. Brush the tops of the buns with egg white and bake them for ten minutes. Turn the temperature down to 350 degrees and envision the fire below burning your intention, your praise, your desires and dreams into the buns. Bake them for another 15 minutes or until they are golden brown. Remove them from the sheet immediately and let them cool on a wire rack.

If you wish, you can glaze the buns by whisking together 1⅓ cups powdered sugar and 2 tablespoons milk. Spoon the glaze over the warm buns, allowing it to run into the cross. As you eat your bun, envision yourself taking in the abundance that the goddess grants to the blessed land. Share this special springtime treat with your beloveds. What you send out will be returned to you.

BELTANE

THE FERTILE EARTH

HAILED AS THE beginning of summer, Beltane is usually celebrated on April 30 or May 1. The flowers of the hawthorn tree are in bloom; the mantle of spring's culmination and summer's advent beautifies the radiant earth. Winter's chains are broken for good as the wheel of the year turns from winter to summer. Love is in the air as bee carries pollen from blossom to aromatic blossom and honey drips from the comb. The sacred union of the goddess and the god is observed, and sexuality is celebrated as we regard our bodies as mirrors of the divine plan. The blazing flames of the great bonfire mirror the passion within our hearts. The tenderness of the new spring season transforms before our eyes into the lush fullness of new life taking hold and thriving. Everywhere, in root and in flower, the proliferation of abundance on the earth is seen. Great fires are ignited, and the door to the Otherworld opens once again.

The veneration of fire associated with Beltane is believed by many to have originated with the worship of the Celtic sun god Belenus. Likened to the Greek god Apollo, the name *Belenus* has been interpreted to mean "bright shining one" and is often considered to be the etymological derivative for *Beltane*. *Beltane* or *Là Beltaine*, as it is also known, can be broken down into *là*, meaning "day," *bel* as a reference to the god, and *taine* (fire).

Belenus appears frequently in mythology, suggesting that his worship was pervasive. He was revered primarily at freshwater springs and has been associated with healing as well as with solar energy. The Celts believed that by night, the sun traveled underneath the world to heat the waters in the thermal springs, uniting the energy of the sun with the healing properties of water. In name, Belenus is linked to the Celtic goddess Belisima, who is associated with the cosmos, with rivers, and the solar flame. Belisima shares many characteristics associated with the goddess Brighid. Both appear to be unique Celtic deities in that their worship was not confined to one specific geographical area. Additionally, both Brighid and Belisima are associated with healing, water, and fire.

THE GREAT FIRE OF BELTANE

Beltane was celebrated as the beginning of summer and the beginning of the seasonal cycle of planting and grazing. The festival begins on Beltane eve, as the hearth fires are extinguished and then relit from the bonfire blazing upon the nearest hill. This ritual arose from the practical agricultural necessity of burning off the old brush before rendering the pastures suitable for use. Cattle were driven around and between the bonfires to ensure their health and to ward off pestilence as they were moved from their protected winter pastures back up to the green mountains where they would remain until Samhain.

In addition to their agricultural significance, cattle also had a divinatory role at Beltane. The appearance of a white heifer was considered very auspicious, a manifestation of Bóand, goddess of inspiration and abundance who is credited with establishing the fertile *Bru nà Boinne*, the Boyne River Valley in County Meath, Ireland. Her presence signified an assurance of human health as well as the good health of the cattle. One of her particular associations is the white cow. In Nordic culture, Beltane was referred to as *thrimilci*—the day upon which cows could be milked three times in one day.

The tradition of the Beltane fires survived in Wales until the 1840s, while in Ireland, where the tradition of the Beltane bonfire began, the practice continued into the mid-twentieth century. And in Scotland to this very day, the Beltane Fire Society holds an annual bonfire, invoking rituals from days long past. Like Samhain, Beltane is a sabbat wherein it is believed that the door to the spirit world is open, or that the veil in between the worlds is thin enough for spirits to pass through. But unlike Samhain, which is a festival of the dead, Beltane is a festival of the living. And wandering spirits on Beltane are believed to be seeking much more than a visit or a meal. More likely, they are seeking incarnation or, alternately, intercourse with the living.

The sexual license often attributed to faeries or spirits seemed to have an influence on the behavior of human mortals as well. The young men and women who ventured out into the woods

Legends and Lore
The Arrival of the Gods

The first of May is a date that carries great significance in Celtic lore. In addition to the lighting of the Beltane fires, May 1 is acknowledged as the date on which the first of the ancient deities crossed over from the Otherworld to land in Ireland. The race of Partholón, as they were called, flourished along with the land. During the 300 years of Partholónic propagation, the island of Ireland was said to have increased in surface area and in the number of lakes. The Partholóns were the enemies of the Fomors, a race of demons who represented evil, darkness, and death. They battled ferociously, and the people of Partholón ultimately triumphed against them. By defeating Cichol, the leader of the Fomors, Partholón is credited with ushering in 300 years of peace.

The peaceful reign of the race of Partholón, which began with twenty-four men and twenty-four maidens, also tragically ended on the first of May. A mysterious plague, lasting for a week, killed all 5,000 of Partholón's people. As if they sensed their oncoming doom, they gathered together on their first created plain of Ireland where they originally landed in order for any survivors to easily facilitate funerary rites for the stricken. Possibly for this reason, Beltane is also considered sacred to Bilé, the Celtic god of death.

on May Eve under the auspices of gathering flowers with which to celebrate May Day frequently succumbed to passion. The Puritans are reputed to have had particular disdain for Beltane observances, and documented such complaints that of all the young ladies who went "a-maying" not one of them returned a virgin.

Such "greenwood weddings" were common and were perhaps influenced by local custom as much as by licentious cavorting spirits. In Britain, a May Queen was crowned with flowers and then married to the May King in a symbolic joining of the fertile powers of the land. The May Queen represented the transformation of the blossoming maiden into the Mother Goddess. This divine transformation is reflected in the earthly rite of sexual awakening. The overtly phallic symbology of the maypole was apparent, as the cut tree (most often a young sapling) was brought from the woods, stripped, and plunged into a hole in the earth, prominently displayed in the town square. The blatant sexual suggestiveness of this custom was not lost on the early Puritans, who outlawed the maypole in 1644.

Since Beltane originated as an agricultural festival, it makes sense that weather divination would play an important role in its observance. Temperature and precipitation were believed to be omens for the harvest. Frost on Beltane was interpreted as ominous, while a rainy day predicted good fortune and a bountiful harvest. Additionally, a reverence for flowers and greenery characterized typical Beltane customs. Gathering flowers and adorning a "may bush" with ribbons, brightly colored fabric, and blossoms was a custom that prevailed in Ireland up until the nineteenth century.

127

Together with Imbolc and Lughnasad, Beltane was the day upon which holy wells were visited the most. The well is representative of the female principle, where an observer can directly experience the life-giving powers that arise from the mysterious depths of the earth. Devotees would execute the pattern walk, that is, walking deosil around the well, offering up silent prayers for health and healing.

Alternately, the petitions were written on fabric and ribbon and tied to the boughs of trees. Of all the trees reputed to possess magical properties, the hawthorn, ash, thorn, and sycamore held the greatest importance at Beltane, as these were the trees thought most likely to provide a conduit between the petitioner and the deities. Another common pattern walk typically carried out on or around Beltane was the custom of walking along the boundaries of one's property as a method of invoking protection. "Beating the bounds" was a pattern walk wherein members of an entire community would walk the boundaries of their parish, usually led by a minister.

In Rome, Beltane coincided with the standing festival of Floralia, which began on April 28 and typically lasted until May 1 or 3, by varying accounts. The Floralia was the commemoration of Flora, goddess of flowers and fruit, capable of bestowing vitality and youth. Sabine in origin, Flora was introduced to the Romans by Titus Tatius. Spring and its abundant blossoms were her tokens, and she was celebrated with grand theatrics. Flora was credited with controlling the prosperity of all fruits, trees, and flowers. Sexual indiscretion was another customary method of celebrating her power.

In Ireland, the first of May is the date upon which the Tuatha Dé Danaan are believed to have arrived from Scotland. The Tuatha Dé Danaan were the fourth of the ancient races of divinity believed to have populated the island before the arrival of man. They were skilled magicians and introduced the art of metalworking. For 200 years, they flourished. The Tuatha Dé Danaan were finally defeated by the Milesians and took up residence in the hills of Ireland. There, they are reputed to have diminished in size and became the *sidhe,* or faerie folk.

Celestial Events
THE SCALES OF LIBRA

Looking to the southeast horizon, we may see the constellation Libra making its first appearance in the night sky in early May. The Celts honored the principles of polarities and opposites, as is evident in the way they divided the year in half, marking the turning points from winter to summer with bonfires, festivals, and divination. What better constellation to embody polarity than the scales of Libra!

129

Libra was once considered to be a part of Scorpius but was classified as a separate constellation by the Romans when the Julian calendar was established. It is unique among the zodiac signs in that Libra is the only one represented by an inanimate object, the scales of balance. In Arabic, the names of the two brightest stars in Libra translate as "southern claw" (Zuben el Genubi) and "northern claw" (Zuben Eschamali), attesting to its former association with the claws of the scorpion. The southern claw star lies almost directly on the ecliptic and can be located by establishing the visual halfway point between Spica and Antares, the "eye" of Scorpius, visible above the southeast horizon at about 10:00 P.M.

Later, the scales of Libra were linked to the goddess Astraea. A goddess of justice, Astraea was the daughter of Zeus and Themis. Her name means "star maiden," and her association with justice probably stems from her parentage. Zeus, as father of the gods, carried great power, and his coupling with Themis, whose name has been interpreted both as "divine justice" and "due order," imparted particular gifts upon their immortal daughter.

During the Golden Age, Astraea lived on earth (as did all the deities) and bestowed her blessings upon its inhabitants. At the end of the age, when mankind was deemed too wicked to enjoy the direct presence of the gods, she was the last of the deities to leave earth for heaven. She reveals her scales in the night sky to remind the mortals below that she will one day return to us and measure out her justice.

Astrological Influences

THE REIGN OF TAURUS AND THE AGE OF INNOCENCE

The sacred bull is an icon that appears in diverse mythologies across thousands of years and survives to this day in the constellation Taurus. The bull features prominently in the cosmology of Mesopotamia, in the Persian Mithraic cult, and the cult of the Minotaur in Crete. Perhaps no other animal has been so closely linked with gods and goddesses alike.

From the sacred bull of Mithras, whose death created the cosmos, to the bull that slaughtered Tammuz, the consort of the goddess Ishtar, setting into motion the cycle of seasons, the bull is strongly identified with the genesis and fertility of the land. Sensuality without shame and beauty in the absence of vanity are the hallmarks of Taurus. The innocence of Taurus can be experienced by observing any young child or blossoming youth who has not yet learned to be ashamed of nakedness. A fixed earth sign, Taurus carries a negative charge and a decidedly feminine energy. Its association with the planet named for the goddess of love serves as an amplifier of the power of Beltane. The horns of the bull were equated with the horns of the crescent moon, hence its association with the lunar goddess. The many goddesses associated with Taurus include Isis, Aphrodite, Io, Maeve, and Selene.

Another trait popularly associated with Taurus is the presence of artistic ability. This association may have arisen from the fact that some of the earliest known art in existence features images of the wild caattle, or aurocs, the predecessor of the modern domestic cattle. The paintings of aurochs in the caves of Lascaux in southwest France are believed to have been created sometime between 13,000 and 25,000 B.C. Their presence attests to the great significance of bulls in Paleolithic culture. Furthermore, the Sumerian *Epic of Gilgamesh* includes a reference to the sacrilege of bull slaughter: Such an act was considered offensive to the gods. Taurus can easily be viewed as a representation of the Bull of Heaven, referenced in the *Epic of Gilgamesh*, which is regarded as the oldest article of recorded history.

Tropical astrology holds the sun to enter Taurus on April 21 and remain until May 21, bringing the energy of the sun through this Venus-ruled constellation to the Beltane fires. Folklorists consider the true date of Beltane to occur when the sun is at 15 degrees Taurus, giving the sabbat an astrological calendar date that will vary somewhat from year to year. In astronomy, the sun is in Aries on Beltane. This modern association is a powerful one because Aries emanates the only passion intense enough to even approach love. The passion of war can be viewed as the opposite of love, bringing the balance of polarities into play. Furthermore, Aries is a consort of Aphrodite, the supreme goddess of love and sexuality, and father to Eros, the god of erotic love. Both Aries and Taurus have profound implications on Beltane. The arcane astrological observances resonate with the current path of the sun through the zodiac.

Meditation
THE SACRAL CHAKRA

One of the aspects of Wicca that sets it apart from most other religions is beautifully illustrated in a single line of the oracle commonly known as "The Charge of the Goddess," wherein the goddess states, "All acts of love and pleasure are mine." When many other commonly accepted spiritual paths place so much emphasis on asceticism and sacrifice, it can be a challenge to fully embrace the sentiment of pleasure as a form of religious expression. The goddess does not demand sacrifice of her devotees; rather, she invites us to love. And while fasting and deprivation can certainly prelude a mystical experience, it is important to recognize that a spiritual revelation can just as equally be accompanied by sensuality. Think of love and pleasure not just in terms of gratification, but as divine gifts from the goddess who claims them as her own.

Love is a powerful emotion and has been called "the calling card of the goddess." It is often in the pursuit of love that devotees discover her and are motivated to call on her for aid. Whether it concerns one person making room in his or her life for another or a love-struck worshipper seeking divine intervention in securing another's affection, the goddess has always been invoked by those seeking her assistance in promulgating amorous desires.

133

Before we can love another, we must first love ourselves. One cannot hope to give what one does not already possess. This exercise is designed to align desire with action so that self-love is radiated outward to the world. What is sent out is returned to the sender threefold. This meditation can be performed alone or with a partner. Take some time to read through the entire exercise before you attempt it. You will need to do some advance preparation in gathering items that appeal to each of your five senses.

Start by giving yourself some protected, sacred space. Turn off the ringer on your telephone, lock the door, and take some time to clear your mind. Claim this time as an hour or two just for yourself, a time for focusing on your desire, honoring yourself, and experiencing the delights of the senses. Take as much time as you can. Do not rush.

A good way to begin is with aromatic incense. Take some sandalwood and add a few drops of jasmine oil. Burn it on a charcoal placed in a shell. The combined ingredients will gently smolder. Set the shell on the ground and sit in a chair with your legs extended outward, letting the smoke weave its way between your toes.

Take up the shell and gently wave it back and forth in front of your whole body. Place it on a table in front of you and with both hands, gently fan the smoke to your face and over your head. As you do this, whisper the words, "By the smoke I am caressed. By the goddess I am blessed."

Take a drop of the jasmine oil and anoint your forehead in a small clockwise circle, right about where you picture your third eye to be (usually the center of the forehead, above and between the eyes), with these words: "With the kiss of the goddess upon my head, blessed be my body and blessed be my bed." Know that jasmine was considered sacred to the goddess Ishtar. Jasmine blossoms, while very fragrant, are also very delicate and difficult to cultivate. Enjoy this sensory indulgence to its fullest.

Next, choose some music to listen to. It can be romantic and dreamy or up-tempo and invigorating. The most important thing is that the music fit your mood and that you are wildly passionate about it. Whether you are inspired by classical masters or Top 40, pick something dramatic that gets your blood flowing. As you listen to the music, think about what it is that attracts you to the sound. Is it a repetitive driving rhythm, or the many layers of a complicated arrangement? Explore your own musical tastes as a method for achieving greater self-awareness. Do you find song lyrics evocative, or do you prefer instrumental compositions? Let the music take you down its sacred path, for music is indeed sacred. It is a universal language spoken in times of celebration. Celebrate yourself and let your music play the soundtrack of your spirit for your ears to enjoy.

William Shakespeare described music as the food of love, and it is inspiring to think that music nourishes love. It is also important to nourish your body as well. Throughout history, mankind has sought all manner of edible aphrodisiacs in order to provoke love into fruition. Oysters were believed to provide sexual enhancement because of their derivation from the sea, which was the birthplace of Aphrodite, the Greek goddess of sexuality and love. All foods that come from the bounty of the ocean are thought to contain traces of her sexy essence. Almonds, too, have been

By Many Names

Bealtaine, Là Beltain, May Eve, May Day, Galan-Mai, and Cétshamain are some of the other names by which Beltane is known.

considered an aphrodisiac, perhaps because the almond shell is the silhouette of the yoni, the sacred emblem of the feminine genitalia. The bright orange color of the mango fruit resonates with the sacral chakra, the center of sexuality, and the mango is also said to enhance desire. Chocolate is equally famous for its endorphin-releasing effects as it is for its delicious taste.

Choose something that makes your taste buds come alive and your mouth nice and juicy. Prepare something special in advance, or just go to the refrigerator or the cupboard and take out your favorite indulgence. Think about its symbolism or implications, if there are any obvious ones. Whatever flavor you choose to engage, the most important thing is not the food's aphrodisiac properties, but how you experience taste. Sweet or salty, hot or cold doesn't matter. What matters is that you love it.

Prepare a delicious beverage for yourself as well. Hold the liquid on your tongue to savor it before you swallow. Think about why you like what you like. What is it about your favorite food and drink that you find so appealing? Is it the way sweetness spreads across your tongue or the salty bite that commands your attention? Enjoy your chosen indulgence and the pleasure that it brings.

Now it is time to indulge your tactile senses. What are you wearing? Does the feel of the fabric please you? If not, then change! Find something irresistible, something that makes you want to run your hands over it again and again. Get comfortable. Whether it is the smoothness of satin, the softness of suede, or the gossamer fibers of silk that activate your sense of touch, find something tactile that truly pleases you. And do not stop with what you

merely have on. Explore the softness and comfort of plump pil-
lows or a fine blanket. Maybe there is a particular texture that you
find especially pleasing. If nothing immediately comes to mind,
take some time for discovery. Your body will let you know.

Now take a look around you. Certainly you have accumulated some things that please you. Did you paint your room in
your favorite colors? Does your altar contain certain objects that
you felt drawn to, more for their aesthetic nature than anything
else? Do you decorate your walls with prints or artwork? Think
about the things that stimulate you visually. Are you drawn to
color? Certain patterns? A particular artist, or theme? Allow
your gaze to fall upon a vision that pleases you and take in the
beauty while contemplating its significance. Think of all the
wonders of nature that we experience visually: the stunning colors of the sunset, the luminous pastels of spring blossoms, the
myriad hues of the rainbow. Visual stimulation is all around you.
It is also within you. While it is pleasurable to take in the beauty
of the world with your eyes, you can also focus on inner beauty
by using creative visualization to assist in opening the sacral
chakra.

The chakras are generally described as being the "organs"
of the ethereal body. Just as each one of us possesses a physical
form, so too are we believed to possess an accompanying spiritual form. Some people have the gift of being able to physically
see these emanations of the spirit in the form of auras and the
like. These spiritual forms contain energy centers located along
the column of the spine. When they are in alignment, they can
have a substantial impact on spiritual wellness that manifests in

how one experiences and relates to the world. To open a chakra center is to allow yourself to experience a greater range of possibilities. The sacral chakra is most closely associated with the realm of pleasure, desire, and sexuality. It is located just below the navel and its corresponding color is orange.

Sit with your spine very straight and envision an orange pinpoint of light emanating from your sacral chakra. Allow the light to grow until it surrounds you in a glowing embrace of stimulating serenity. It is possible, even desirable, to be both relaxed and invigorated at the same time. With your mind's eye, picture a circle. Let images flow freely as you think of all the things that a circle can represent: the earth, the sun, the moon, the protection

Spell for Beltane Beauty

It was believed that the morning dew of May 1 held special powers. Maidens would gather the dew from plants and anoint their faces with it, believing it would increase their physical attractiveness. Some ladies were also known to disrobe and roll around in the morning dew, allowing it to cover their entire bodies in order to extract the greatest effectiveness from its beautifying power. Others would run a silver spoon across the grass and bottle the dew. You can imitate this custom by gathering a few dew-soaked leaves on Beltane morning and suspending them in a container of purified spring water. Pour the water into a misting bottle and spray over your face and body for a refreshingly simple Beltane observance.

of the circle cast, the turning wheel of the year. It is interesting how the simpler a symbol, the more complex its associations.

Allow the circle to change so that there is a crescent contained within it. Meditate on the crescent. The crescent represents receptivity. It is also the symbol of the new moon. When the moon is new, the stars seem brighter, for they are no longer lost in the radiance of the shining orb. In darkness, beauty is revealed. The crescent is a cradle. A chalice, waiting to be filled. Think of the things you would most like to call toward yourself.

As you picture your desires being fulfilled, the circle with the crescent inside becomes a blossom. Slowly unfolding around the outer perimeter are six lotus petals. Picture them gently opening all at once, opening you to the possibility of your desires coming into being. Concentrate on your own worthiness. Cultivate confidence and radiate self-assurance and self-worth to the world. When opportunity presents itself, you will be ready. By taking the time to engage all of your senses, you have no doubt learned a few things about yourself in the process. And with knowledge comes power.

139

Ritual
LOVE SPELLS FOR BELTANE

With its accompanying themes of sexual union and pleasure-seeking, Beltane is an ideal time for enacting spells to draw one's heart's desire nearer to one's self. It is only natural that we may wish to emulate the sacred union of goddess and god by reflecting romantic coupling in our own lives. While there is nothing wrong with naming your heart's desire and using your craft to assist in bringing a desired outcome into being, it is important to do so in accordance with the will of the universe and refrain from any type of attempted manipulation of affection.

Think of the spell as uncovering the love that is there and assisting its emergence, and not a means of seducing a person against their will or calling into being something that is not meant to exist. While manipulative magic may indeed produce results, most often these results are fleeting and rebound on the sender in an undesired and unanticipated way. It is also important to have a sense of what is realistic when enacting a spell. Trying to enact a love spell to gain the affection of a celebrity whom you are not likely to meet is unrealistic, no matter how strong your desire may be.

A love spell is best begun on the new moon, with a simple ritual observed each night as the moon waxes, culminating on the full moon when the energy is sent out into the universe. Allow the energy of Beltane to act as an amplifier to the work at hand. Begin with two red candles, signifying passion. A pair of male and female effigy candles or two tapered candles will work best. On the first one, inscribe your name, date of birth, and astrological glyph. Take some copal resin and crush it in your mortar and pestle so that it becomes a fine powder. Rub the powder in the inscriptions so that they are visible. On the second candle, carve the name, date of birth, and astrological glyph of your desired one. Repeat the application of copal powder to bring out the carvings. Females place the first candle, which represents the self, on the left side of the altar. Place the second candle, which represents your desire, on the right side. Males reverse the placements. Place your wand horizontally across your altar. Symbolic of the power of the will, this important tool is used to help bring your will into being. Burn the remainder of the copal on a charcoal as an offering to Aphrodite and ask for her assistance:

"Stately Aphrodite, born from the gentle foam of the sea
She who encompasses divine beauty and inspires love in the
hearts of men
Mother to the god of love, who embodies feminine perfection,
Hear the desire of your faithful devotee.
I call for your aid in revealing the love between myself
and _____
That our bond may be an earthly reflection of your loveliness
and blessing.
By your grace, may the sacred union of heart and hand be ours."

Light your candles and meditate on your fondest desire coming true. Allow yourself to visualize the highest possibility and best outcome. Speak the following charm as you gaze into the candles' glow:

"May the goddess hear my plea
If this love is meant to be
Turn my lover's heart to me
By all the power of three times three
As I do will, so mote it be."

141

Pinch out the candle flames with your thumb and forefinger. As the moon waxes, repeat the spell, moving the two candles a little closer together each night. On the night of the full moon, let the two candles burn down together. Gather the cooled wax and release it into a body of moving water.

Charm to Invoke Love

With its themes of sexuality and union, Beltane is a powerful time for love magick. Here, you will find a simple but effective charm for invoking love. You will need these things:

Two pieces of red felt, about 4 inches square
Two pieces of paper measuring 4 inches by 6 inches
A pen with red ink
A copper coin, such as a penny
A cowrie shell (or other small seashell)
Needle and thread

Take the first piece of paper and fold it in half lengthwise. Using a pair of scissors, cut out one lobe of a heart shape starting from the folded edge. This will give you a perfect template for cutting two heart shapes out of the red felt. As you cut out the two hearts, focus on one heart representing you and the other representing the one you desire.

On the second piece of paper, write your intended's name on both sides, as many times as will fit. The repetition of this task will sharpen your focus and may even become trancelike. Fold the paper around the coin until it is very small and will

Ride of the Witches

The Germanic people referred to Beltane as Walpurgisnacht. On Walpurgisnacht, all of the witches would gather on the Brocken, the highest peak of the Hartz Mountains, for their revels. At the summit of the Brocken there was reputed to be a spring and a consecrated altar used in the witches' ceremonies. As late as 1751, the summit of the Brocken was referred to as "Witches' Ground" and was even indicated on some German maps by the inclusion of flying witches, who would reputedly fly on broomsticks, instilling fear and terror in those who were not of their kind. The besom is a highly charged emblem of sexuality, as it resembles the union of male and female genitalia. Goethe describes the lively revels in this excerpt from *Faust*:

> *The witches ride to the Brocken's top*
> *The stubble is yellow, and green is the crop*
> *There gathers the crowd for carnival . . .*
> *Then honor to whom the honor is due*
> *Dame Baubo first, to lead the crew!*
> *A tough old sow and the mother thereon*
> *Then follow the witches, every one . . .*

The reference to Baubo alludes to the mourning of Demeter at the loss of her daughter, Persephone. Baubo was the only one who had the ability console the goddess in her profound grief. Baubo's lascivious appearance (she is usually depicted as a walking female torso with breasts for eyes, her navel as her nose, and genitalia for her mouth) lifted Demeter's spirits.

fit between the two hearts. Lay the cowrie on top of the folded paper and set all of the objects between the hearts.

Sew them together, envisioning the two hearts becoming one. The folded paper represents your desire, the copper coin is the conductor to carry your intention to the goddess, and the cowrie shell is the goddess symbol. Sleep with the charm under your pillow until your love manifests.

Practical Craft
CONSTRUCTING A MAYPOLE

The symbolism of the maypole originated in India, where the sacred phallus was revered as the embodiment of the divine male principle. United with the earth as a symbolic gesture to ensure the fecundity of the land, the maypole represents the renewal of life and the return of warmth. The maypole is some-times interpreted as a sort of degradation of the World Tree of Norse mythology. The World Tree, or Yggdrasil, as it is called, was a great ash tree whose mighty trunk pierced the earth, connecting life and death, and the earth to heaven. All of the living earth was viewed as a function of its many parts; roots, limbs, branches, and leaves encompassed the entire living world. It was from Yggdrasil that the supreme god Odin suspended himself for nine days. Wounded by his own spear, he hung by his foot and took neither food nor drink during his ordeal. The reward for his suffering was knowledge of the runes, which he spied inscribed on a rock below.

Retaining the significance of the god aspect, the maypole was a common element to May Day celebrations and still survives to this day, albeit more of an innocent secular activity for children than the blatant sexual rites of the past. Today there are two types of maypole dances that remain popular, and each has a specific construction requirement for the maypole.

The first is the simpler of the two, in that the pole can be danced around in no particular order and the pole does not have any specific height requirements. A spinning disc is attached to the top of the pole, and many colored ribbons are hung from it. There should be one ribbon for each participant. The spinning disc can easily be created by taking an embroidery hoop and attaching it to a small ring. Tie the embroidery hoop to the ring with festive ribbon in four equidistant places. You can then tie various lengths of ribbon to the hoop. The ribbons should be almost as long as the pole itself. Once the ribbons are attached to the hoop, drive a long nail halfway into the top of the pole and place the ring over the nail. It is important that the ring have a smaller diameter than the pole or the hoop will just fall off and won't balance atop the pole. Secure the pole into the ground and invite each reveler to take hold of a ribbon (there may be as few as three participants or as many as twelve or twenty). They proceed to dance and skip in a circle, changing directions as a group. This method does not produce a braid around the maypole and does not

145

require any choreography, so it is a suitable exercise for any age group with varying abilities.

The second type of May dance requires a simpler pole, but more complex choreography. It produces a colorful braid as the various ribbons are wound around the pole. The pole has a certain height requirement, in that it should be at least two feet taller than the tallest participant. The ribbons should be of equal length, and should be as long as the pole is tall. Unlike the previously described maypole, the ribbons in this version are permanently affixed to the top of the pole.

Splay the ribbons out in a star pattern, overlapping them at one end, and then driving a single nail through the center of the ribbons and into the center of the top of the pole. Make sure the ribbons are secure and do not move, otherwise it will be impossible to produce the braid. Raise the pole and secure it into the ground, at least a foot deep to ensure that it will not topple over. There should ideally be an even number of participants. Each takes hold of a ribbon and one person stands, while the next person kneels, alternating around the circle. Two side-by-side participants begin the dance by facing in opposite directions, and then weaving in and out of the standing and kneeling participants. When they return to their original positions, one will stand and the other will kneel, and the next two side-by-side dancers will weave around the circle. The process is repeated until the ribbons are wrapped around the pole as far as they will go.

Season Six

LITHA

SUMMER'S SONG

THE SPROUTING LEAVES are now dense and thick as flower gives way to ripening fruit. Usually occurring on or around June 21, the sabbat of Litha is the triumph of the sun and the culmination of the Green Man or the Oak King, the embodiment of the spirit of nature and the sacred male principle. His strength is at its most potent before he is cut down in a symbolic sacrifice representing the necessity of death in order for life to continue, anticipating the coming of the harvest. He is the wild soul that revels in the fullness of nature. His visage appears among the lush green leaves, peering out from among the foliage with penetrating eyes that shine forth with the wisdom of the natural world. He signifies the chaos and beauty of the potent god; he is the natural order of the universe and the frenzy of life untamed.

Sharing similarities with Beltane, Litha is a sabbat strongly associated with elemental fire.

In an effort to assist the sun in changing its course, great bonfires were lit. Oftentimes, the midsummer bonfire escaped
its bounds, as devotees would hurl flaming discs at the sun or,
alternately, roll burning wheels down the hillside. Litha is also
characterized by the presence of the faerie realm. Contact with
the faeries, desirable and dangerous at once, is possible at this
time. Midsummer's Eve was often regarded as a time of intense
magic and was considered suitable for casting love spells and
charms. Any herbs gathered at midnight on Midsummer's Eve
were believed to have unparalleled potency.

THE SUMMER SOLSTICE

The sun reaches the point on the celestial sphere where it is
again at the greatest distance from the celestial equator, only
this time the earth is tilted its full 23.5 degrees in the direction
of the sun. The sun shines directly over the Tropic of Cancer, at
a latitude 23 degrees north, and seems to stop for a moment as
the earth's journey around the sun reaches a culmination. The
sun will be at its farthest north along the horizon, standing still
before beginning its slow return to the southern sky.

In Great Britain, standing stark on the hill of Salisbury
Plain, are the megaliths of Stonehenge. What appear to be the
remnants of great dolmen arches stand as they have for 5,000
years, a mysterious enigma that has never been solved. One
indisputable fact about Stonehenge is that the circle of stones
and the great avenue leading to its center is in alignment with

the summer solstice sunrise. Whether Stonehenge was intended as a calendar, timepiece, observatory, or ritual space remains debated to this day. But also to this day, the sun does not fail to fall upon the Heel Stone, casting a lingering shadow on the morning of the summer solstice and again on the evening of the winter solstice.

The summer solstice was considered sacred to the Celtic goddess Danu, or Anu as she was alternately known. As goddess, she would bestow fertility, prosperity, and abundance. Her followers would circle her sacred ground of Cnoc Aine carrying torches of straw and hay. Waving the torches over themselves, their cattle, and their crops, they sought to secure her blessing and her aid.

When the day is at its longest and the full glory of the earth is manifested in the bounty of summer, every rock, tree, bird, and insect seems to radiate vitality. A whirl of activity takes place before the coming darkness. We take a cue from the natural world and use this time to align with the powerful energies that surround us. While the summer solstice is a culmination, it is also an ending. As the power of the sun reaches its peak, the only thing that can follow is decline. This penultimate surge of strength precedes death. The time of the Oak King, the half-year of burgeoning life and light, passes and the reign of the Holly King, who presides over the waning year, begins.

Origin of the Faeries

In Celtic mythology, the goddess Danu was hailed as the universal mother. She is considered the most ancient Celtic

149

divinity and is the mother of the Tuatha Dé Danaan. Her consort was Bilé, the god seen as the first ancestor of the Tuatha Dé Danaan, and sometimes referred to as a father of men. Also called Anu or Ana, Danu represented the earth and all of its fruitfulness. Her children were the early gods of the land. One of her sons was Nuada, the supreme god of war. Nuada is likened to a Celtic version of Zeus and was king of the Tuatha Dé Danaan (although, unlike his Grecian counterpart, he is noted more for his exploits in battle than for amorous liaisons).

The Tuatha Dé Danaan arrived upon the island of Ireland concealed within great clouds of mist and dense fog. For this reason, they were able to establish themselves unbeknownst to the reigning tribes of the Fir Bolgs. They are described as unparalleled in beauty and magical ability. The Tuatha Dé Danaan were mighty warriors, adept artisans, and possessed the power of enchantment. They descended onto the island, some say from earth, others from heaven, sending showers of blood and fire across the plains, causing the Fir Bolgs to retreat and seek cover. Legend has it that the Fir Bolgs grew wise to their enchantment and issued a series of magical counterattacks to break the charm.

Finally, on Midsummer's Day, the two armies met and launched a series of deadly battles. The fighting lasted four days and ended with the death of Eochaid, the Fir Bolg king, and the wounding of Nuada. He lost his hand in combat and was consequently deposed, for a blemished king was considered unfit for the throne. An alliance was struck with another race of gods, the Fomors. Bres Mac Elatha would become the new leader of the Tuatha Dé Danaan; however, due to his Fomorian heritage, his rule would favor the race of his descent, setting the stage for the next war between gods.

The Tuatha Dé Danaan possessed a formidable army as skilled at fighting with incantation and poetry as they were with spear and shield. Led by the Dagda, Ogma, and Lugh, the divine Tuatha Dé Danaan were able to suppress the tyrannical Fomorian rule until their ultimate defeat at the hands of a most unlikely enemy: an invading army of mortal men.

The Milesians most likely would not have been able to overcome the Tuatha Dé Danaan without the assistance of the druid, Amergin. He was the first to set foot on Ireland's shore when Mile arrived with his sons, their wives, and a battalion of thirty-six chiefs, each accompanied by scores of warriors. He uttered a ballad and proceeded to subdue the Tuatha Dé Danaan with his magical arts. He won the alliance of the wind, the sea, and the land, enabling the Milesian armies to ultimately depose and kill the three kings of the Tuatha Dé Danaan.

The Tuatha Dé Danaan ultimately decided to abandon the surface of the land and retreat underground. There, they became the *daoine sidhe,* the people of the hills, and every god and goddess became a faerie. They divided the hills of Ireland among themselves, so that not a one of them was without a kingdom. They never surrendered their divine powers and could often be found to lend aid to or alternately discombobulate human affairs, as they saw fit.

Celestial Events
THE HERO, THE DRAGON, AND THE CROWN

The sky at midsummer is a treasure trove of mythological lore. From the virulent conquering male hero of Greek mythology to the Babylonian genesis myth, the stars above continue to remind us of the link between mortals and the deities, projecting the age-old legends in the language of their sparkling light.

Hercules

At around 10:30 P.M., the constellation Hercules will be visible at the zenith, its most recognizable feature the central "box" made up of four stars in a trapezoid pattern. Hercules, or Herakles, was by far the most famous of all the Greek heroes. He was a son of Zeus and Alkmene and, by way of his divine and illegitimate parentage, incurred the persistent wrath of Hera, the often-maligned wife of Zeus. Renowned for completion of the legendary Twelve Labors, Hercules was worshipped as a god throughout the Mediterranean.

Just as enthralling as the exploits of his life are the circumstances surrounding his death. While living in exile with his wife Deianira, Hercules shot and killed the centaur Nessus to protect his wife from rape. As the centaur lay dying, he offered Deianira his blood to be used as a love charm should Hercules' affection ever turn away from her. Deianira gathered the charm, not knowing that Nessus' blood contained not a love charm but rather the instrument of the centaur's revenge. Deianira eventually did suspect that Hercules had eyes for another woman, and she applied the dried blood to one of his robes in an effort to turn his heart back to her. When Hercules put on the robe, it burned his skin. When he removed the robe, his skin was removed with it. When Deianira learned that instead of arousing Hercules' affection she had burned him alive, she was overcome with remorse and committed suicide.

Awash with grief at the death of his wife, Hercules built her a funeral pyre and mounted it himself. In a great flash of lightning, the entire contents of the pyre were consumed, leaving no trace of its sorrowful passengers. It was widely inferred that Hercules was assumed to Mount Olympus whole and placed in the heavens, as no earthly trace of him remained. As the great midsummer bonfires burn, we are reminded of the power of fire to transform the mortal into the celestial. Let the stars above be a reminder of the ancient flames that once carried a hero to heaven.

Draco: The Celestial Dragon

Directly north of Hercules, you will find Draco, the celestial dragon writhing across the night sky. The head of the dragon lies just beneath the hero's feet and its body undulates between Ursa Minor and Ursa Major in a serpentine pattern. Associated with the goddess Athena, the dragon depicted in Draco is associated with the myth of Cadmus and the founding of Thebes. After Cadmus defeated the dragon, he was instructed by Athena to plant the creature's teeth into the ground. Cadmus did so, and from the dragon's teeth sprung full-grown men who assisted him in building the city.

Around 2800 B.C., the pole star was in fact a star in the body of the dragon. The star Thuban, the third bright star from the end of the dragon's tail, was closest to the pole of the earth's axis. Due to precession, the pole star today is Polaris, in Ursa Minor. It is believed by many that the Great Pyramid of Giza was aligned with Thuban at the time of its building.

Another association of Draco is with Tiamat, the primordial dragon of Babylonian mythology. Tiamat was a fearsome monster that represented the ocean depths. She was called the mother of all gods and the mother of all life, just as the sea is often referred to as the cradle of life on earth. Tiamat was killed by the god Marduk, and her death marked the end of chaos and the establishment of heaven and earth. One half of her body became the dome of heaven, the other became the earth below. It is said that her weeping eyes transformed into the Tigris and Euphrates rivers.

In Celtic myth, dragons were the guardians of the land. In the east, the dragon symbolized wisdom. Some interpret the slaying of Tiamat to represent the subjugation of the goddess at the emergence of patriarchy. Likewise, medieval tales of the decimation of dragons at the hands of knights are referenced as the triumph of the culture of death over the ancient wisdom of the goddess. Although our cultural landscape has been dominated by patriarchy, know that the goddess lives and is presently being restored by those who seek to honor the ancient mysteries of her worship. Just as the summer grass will one day fade, it will also surely rise again.

Corona Borealis: Ariadne's Crown

If you turn to face the north, lying to the west of Hercules, you will find an enchanting crescent of seven stars curving upwards. This is the Corona Borealis, the Northern Crown, or the Crown of Ariadne as it is also known. Corona Borealis has a very distinctive feature in addition to its shape. The bright star Gemma is the unmistakable jewel in this glittering summer constellation.

Ariadne was the daughter of Minos, the ruler of Crete. She fell in love with Theseus, a young man who offered himself as a tribute to the deadly Minotaur, a half-bull, half-human creature that dwelled within the depths of the labyrinth. During the rule of Minos, it was customary for the Athenians to send a delegation of seven men and seven maidens as a sacrifice to the Minotaur. This annual tributary meal was believed to stave off a deadly famine.

Ariadne chose to give Theseus her aid. She provided him with a ball of thread and instructed him to attach one end to the opening of the labyrinth so that unlike so many others who had met their death within its maze, he would be able to return. After defeating the Minotaur, Theseus and Ariadne planned to leave Crete together, but en route to Athens, Theseus abandoned his would-be bride. Such was her beauty that Ariadne attracted the attention of none other than Dionysus. He bestowed upon her the gift of ageless beauty. The Corona Borealis was said to be his wedding gift to her, which Dionysus placed in heaven upon her death.

The ancient Britons referred to the Northern Crown as Caer Arianrod, or the Castle of Arianrod. Arianrod was a maiden goddess of Celtic lore, and the unwitting mother to Llew Llaw Gyffes, the Welsh sun-god. The Corona Borealis is also called

155

Caer Sidi, or "Castle of the Sidhe" in ancient Irish folklore. The early pagan sun kings of Ireland were believed to ascend to Caer Sidi upon their death. As you watch the Crown of Ariadne shine in the midsummer night sky, reflect on the connection between deities and devotees. The best way to describe it is love.

Astrological Influences
THE REIGN OF GEMINI AND THE AGE OF ADOLESCENCE

There is no other sign in the zodiac that illustrates the duality of nature more so than Gemini. The third sign of the zodiac, Gemini is ruled by Mercury and is a positive, masculine sign. Represented by the twins, Gemini represents the unfolding of the adolescent soul, a time of great change. Gemini is reminiscent of the youth and vitality of the fullness of summer with the accompanying angst that comes from the realization of the fleeting nature of the season. Dual nature is the characteristic most strongly associated with Gemini.

Most often in mythology, Gemini is linked to the brothers Castor and Pollux, the sons of Leda. Leda was married to King Tyndareus, but she had an extramarital affair with Zeus. The result was one mortal son, Castor, and one divine, Pollux. Her mortal son was killed during a misadventure involving cattle theft. Pollux, so grieved at his brother's death, petitioned Zeus for death, that he might ever be at his brother's side. Zeus struck a compromise with his bereaved son. He allowed Pollux to exchange a portion of his immortality so that he and Castor would change places, alternating their time between Olympus and the underworld.

The touching sacrifice initiated by Pollux on behalf of his brother is especially poignant at the summer solstice because it is at this time that we acknowledge the surrender of the Oak King to his rival, the Holly King. Most often depicted as adversaries, battling it out for control of the year or, alternately, as rivals for the hand of the goddess, the Oak King and the Holly King can also be viewed simply as manifesting the duality of nature; equal but opposite forces who, like Castor and Pollux, must each be consigned to alternately flourish and falter. One cannot exist without the other, for their fates are inextricably bound. Likewise, they cannot occupy the same space in time. One must always rise as the other falls. Such is the great and timeless drama enacted by the revolving Earth in her journey around the sun.

The Oak King and the Holly King are hardly the only twin souls that deserve contemplation. With the tropical astrological

Legends and Lore: The Fire of Necessity

Bonfires were an important feature of the Midsummer celebration. The ancient Saxon tradition of the *fire of necessity*, or need fire, involved constructing a huge bonfire ignited by friction, never from fuel nor spark from an existing fire. The flames were thought to ward off evil spirits; the higher the flames, the further away evil would be driven. Any food cooked over a need fire was believed to have special healing properties.

sign in Gemini from May 22 until June 21, themes of twinship throughout many pantheons are relevant. Greek mythology personifies the sun and moon through another set of twins. The children of Zeus and Leto—Apollo, the sun god, and his twin sister, Artemis, goddess of the moon—embody the concept of polarity in that they are equal opposites. As the solstice passes, the days begin to grow shorter. Think of day slowly succumbing to night as the reign of Apollo gives way to the time of his sister's dominance.

In the Sumerian mystery cycle, the goddess Inanna must confront her dark sister, Ereshkigal, before life on Earth can be restored. And one of the greatest love stories ever recorded is that of the Egyptian deities, Isis and Osiris, twin sister and brother who fell in love within their mother's womb. In addition to representing the adolescent soul, Gemini manifests the sacred dance of creation, the power of change, and the eternal longing for the soul's companion. Discovering the true nature of one's self can also be accelerated by embracing one's opposite. Consider this underlying influence of the duality of nature projected through Gemini when observing the summer solstice.

158

Meditation
DANCING WITH THE SIDHE

The association with midsummer and faeries is long standing. Artists such as Edward Robert Hughes and the great playwright William Shakespeare have created enchanting masterpieces that depict the intersection of the mortal world with the world of the faeries on Midsummer Eve. Let your imagination carry you to the realm of the *daoine sidhe* on Litha.

● You are climbing up the gentle slope of a grassy green hill. The blades of tall grass are deep green, dense and cool beneath your feet. With every step, you feel the subtle give of the supple earth.

● You arrive at the top and look to the sky. Twilight colors are just beginning to appear in rainbow hues that stretch from horizon to horizon. In the western sky, the great red fireball of the sun emblazons the horizon line with its lingering radiance. It is the eve of the longest day.

● The sun hovers low, as if it were unwilling to descend, almost refusing to succumb to the night. Red and orange light subtly change to blues and purples overhead. And as you look to the eastern horizon, the deep violet of twilight is visible. It is as if night and day are coexisting during this time of gentle transition.

● Around your neck, you wear a sacred charm. It is a smooth stone with a natural hole in it. It hangs from a cord and is cool to the touch. You finger it gently as you walk down the side of the hill to greet the trees growing along the meadow below. Fireflies flit about, illuminating the dusk with tiny yellow-green lanterns that appear and disappear. Day lilies begin to slowly close and the winding moonflowers begin to open. This is a magical time of transition. Cicadas, tree frogs, and crickets provide a riotous soundtrack to the emerging night.

● You search the ground for them and discover a ring of white toadstool mushrooms in your path. The buzzing in your ears takes on a discernable rhythmic beat. The wind picks up. It is almost as if you are hearing voices in the wind, speaking an unintelligible language.

● Your heartbeat quickens. It is aligning with the pulsating rhythms exuded by the creatures of dusk. You are synchronizing with the rushing energy of the nature surrounding you. The voices on the wind grow louder.

● You think you see the fluttering of translucent wings around you. Or perhaps your imagination is playing tricks on you. You can't be sure, but your hearing perceives otherworldly voices, high-pitched and melodious, beckoning you, inviting you to join them. You take a deep breath and step inside the circle of mushrooms.

● Suddenly, your perception changes dramatically. Everywhere you turn, you are surrounded by delicate creatures of light with such varying countenances that not one resembles another, neither in shape nor in size. They are everywhere! Every flower has a dancing companion. The birds have gleeful riders. Every blade of grass has a mischievous smile peeking around it. The air is filled with faeries that seem to inhabit the very wind itself.

● They whirl around you as if you were standing in the center of a tornado. The whispering voices are audible to you now. A preternatural song fills your ears, verses sung in rhyme with a repeating melody that entrances you. You begin to sway and suddenly your feet are being lifted.

● You look down and see a dancing host of faeries literally sweeping you off your feet. You try to avoid any missteps, and soon you are joining in the chaotic dance. Your numinous companions whirl around you, diving in and out of your clothes, darting through your hair. You feel as if they are dancing through your very mind itself.

Everything begins to fall away except for the dance. Your heart pounds in your ears, in perfect synchronization to the magical music that surrounds you. The intensity grows. The sun is long gone. Or is it? You search the sky for something familiar, an anchor to reality. You see a brilliant light. Is it the sun? Could it be daybreak already? Or is it the full moon, shining high overhead? Perhaps you would be able to discern if you were just able to slow down for a moment, but you are dancing with the *sidhe,* and there is no such thing as out of breath or the need for rest.

You are no longer dancing; you have become the dance. You are movement. You are grace. You are the embodiment of creative spontaneity. You feel yourself slowly starting to forget, with every turn, with every leap, every smile, every twist, every peal of hysterical laughter. What did you do before you joined in this dance? You can't remember! And this makes you laugh even harder. How long have you been dancing? You can't tell! Has it been all evening or all week?

Lights move across the sky, colors change, and still you dance with the rhythm of the whirlwind that surrounds you. It does not occur to you to stop. Stars soar past overhead leaving tracers in their wake; a fleeting stellar kaleidoscope for your viewing pleasure.

You search the sky for the pole star but in the next moment, the sky is light again. You throw your arms up to the sun, splaying out your fingers, and rays of warmth shine down upon you like a rain of light. You feel as though the light is pouring through you, fuelling your manic dance. In the midst of the joyous frenzy are gossamer wings, elongated limbs, liquid eyes. As soon as you try to focus on one creature, they change shape and disappear. They will not meet your gaze and it becomes clear to you that eye contact will not be possible.

Even as you meld and unite with the faeries through the dance, you have a sense of being an outsider; you are among them but you are not of them. You feel curious eyes upon you, delicate hands against your skin, musical voices in your ears. You dance with abandon. You dance for every wish you have ever had, every great love, every deep hurt, every dream, desire, achievement, triumph, trial, all that you have endured. Every step on the path that brought you to this moment; for this, you dance.

You have touched a realm where time has no meaning, where ecstasy and expression are the only laws of the land. You are graceful and clumsy all at once. You are spinning out of control but never miss a beat just the same. There is a certain perfection here where all of nature, creatures of the land and of the air, the plants, the flowers, the trees, the birds, and the insects seem indistinguishable from each other. You get the sense that it is the *sidhe* that connect them all. An opalescent flower petal is in fact a faerie wing just as surely as the beak on the bluebird morphs into a faerie profile. The dragonfly has tricks up his sleeve; he is teasing the violets into a game of chase.

Everywhere you look, transmogrification is occurring to the extent that you are losing the ability to determine where one world ends and the other begins. All your life, you have heard stories about the veil in between the worlds. Now you feel as though you are tangled up in it, with one foot in one world and the other foot in the next. All it would take is one more step to pass through and leave the earth forever.

As soon as the thought appears in your head, you realize that this is exactly what your dancing companions are gearing up for. Everything seems to be levitating around you, and you are close to being swept along.

Suddenly, you remember your life before the dance. You remember that you love it, that you desire to see the next sunrise, to feel the rain on your face. You are not ready to leave the earth, and this final faerie flight is not meant for you. There are more experiences in store for you on this side of the veil. Although you are intertwined in a rush of exuberance and wonder, you know that somehow you must extricate yourself from the faerie ring.

You remember the talisman around your neck, the stone you found near the water's edge but dry on the shore. The natural hole through the center of it made it perfect for wearing. You grab hold of it in your left hand and pull it up in front of your face where you can peer through the hole.

163

A dazzling ray of light explodes through the center of the hole. The light rapidly surrounds your body and grabs you. You feel as if you are being pulled right through the stone headfirst. It is happening too fast. There is no time for goodbyes or pleasantries of any kind. You are flying headfirst into the unknown as though you were being pulled through the eye of a flaming needle by the hand of the goddess.

● You land with a thud on the soft green grass, damp with either dew or sweat. You can't tell. You are alone, and it is just before sunset. You watch as the sun completes its descent below the horizon, a fiery ball of red, reluctant to give up its reign of light. Then it drops below the horizon line leaving you alone amidst a ring of white toadstools, breathless in the lingering light.

● How long were you gone? It seems as if absolutely no time has passed at all! How can this be, you wonder to yourself, half expecting to be transformed into an elder by now. Around you are the gentle and familiar sounds of the burgeoning night.

● You feel certain that it will still be the shortest night of the year, and that the dance has finally ended in exactly the same place in time where it began, at least for you. As for your companions, they could be on the other side of the world right now for all you know. And they probably are.

● You turn at last to look behind you. The gently sloping hill of green that you climbed only minutes ago is gone.

164

Ritual

INVOKING THE FAERIES

Given the tumultuous history between the race of mortals and the race of faerie, it is easy to understand the faeries' propensity for mischief. Their divine origin has led them to be characterized as semi-immortals, that is, immortals that have taken on corporeal forms. They have been depicted as having an affinity for humans and possess a longing for human children. Faeries have frequently been known to steal human babies and leave one of their own (the "changeling") in its place. They live in lavish grandeur and adore both music and dance. They are reputed to cast spells and throw "glamours," making things appear other than what they are. They are helpers and tricksters. They are distracters and seducers, sometimes friendly, sometimes malicious. The primary purpose of this rite is to win the favor of the faeries so that they will become attracted to you. Faeries love music and dance, so if you possess these talents, the chances of your success will multiply. But faeries are unpredictable. You can begin winning them over with protracted praise, starting with the more noteworthy individuals. Take caution when invoking the faeries, though, for you are just as likely to call in pandemonium as you are partnership.

Folklore offers many colorful suggestions on methods that may be used to see faeries. The famous faerie ointment, consisting of crushed four-leaf clovers, is said to bestow faerie sight on the person whose eyes are anointed with it. It is also frequently written that faeries themselves choose whether they may be seen by humans, and while certain measures may increase one's chances, ultimately it is up to the little folk alone.

The art of invoking faeries is considered by many to be an art belonging mainly to women and children. Children, particularly those under the age of seven, have a distinct affinity with the faeries, as they have not yet been conditioned to disbelieve their own imagination. Age seven is largely considered to be the "age of reason," the developmental milestone when the childlike wonder at the beauty of the earth is grounded more in reality

165

and less in awe and mystery. Nonetheless, faeries are attracted to innocence, and while it may be a natural characteristic of some people, those who wish to experience faeries can cultivate gentleness and innocence in order to achieve greater success.

With the exception of the rare instances where the faeries choose to reveal themselves unsolicited, consorting with faeries is similar in many ways to casting spells. It is attempted within the context of ritual and requires that the practitioner suspend disbelief in her own abilities. By casting a spell, you are seeking to influence events outside of the sphere of your direct control by eliciting a series of controlled coincidences that suit your own ends. Likewise, when invoking faeries, you must expand your belief in what is possible and desirable. Entertain imagination as an alternate reality. When inspiration manifests, we generally accept it and do not question its source. Whether you view your magic as coming from the goddess or coming from within, you can use your magic to invoke faeries just the same as you use it for divination, meditation, and celebration.

You will need some ritual tools and offerings. For this ritual, and for general practice, it is best if you make your own ritual tools. If you feel that you are unable to do this, you may purchase them, but never haggle over the price. Additionally, certain tools such as the athalme, bolline, or dirk are better off purchased. Avoid receiving any of these items as gifts, for folk legends claim that a gift of a blade may sever the friendship between the giver and the recipient. Furthermore, faeries are predominantly creatures of the air, land, and water. It is exceedingly rare to see a faerie associated with fire. Tools created in a forge should ideally be

made by hands other than yours, because faeries are extremely
sensitive to fire. They are reputed to sense its residual energy
long after any presence of fire has occurred. Metals such as
iron and steel have widely been held to be effective talismans for
repelling faeries. The ritual tools that you will need are these:

Athalme or bolline	*Mirror*
Wand	*Chalice*
Bell	*Mead*

You will also need to prepare some offerings with which to
entice the faeries. Faerie lore repeatedly suggests that faeries
are extremely fond of sweets, particularly cake; hazelnuts and
apples are likewise considered to be tempting. Bring some along,
and a libation as well. Honey mead would be the best choice, but
another sweet natural beverage might suffice.

Choose an outdoor location to enact your ritual. Ideally, it
should be in a wooded area with a stream of running water in the
vicinity. The presence of oak trees is particularly auspicious, as
the faeries have an affinity for oak and acorns. Look around for
any evidence of faerie presence (faerie ring of mushrooms, for
instance) that may increase your chances of success. The most
appropriate time of the month to begin this exercise would be
on the first quarter moon, repeating the ritual each evening, culminating on the eve of the full moon, or during the week leading
up to the summer solstice. The repetition is important, because
those who seek to commune with faeries are rarely successful on
a first attempt. Patience and suspension of disbelief are hallmarks

here. It is best performed as twilight approaches, for the faeries are considered to be especially active at this time of day.

Cast a circle with your athalme and call the quarters using the wand to invoke. Set before you the mirror, the chalice of mead, and the bell. Begin the ritual with an invocation to Danu:

"I invoke the goddess Danu. In the bounty of your green woods I stand to pay you homage. Most beautiful Danu the wind picks up your hair and alights it above in a sparkling shower of golden rays containing the shining suns of many worlds. Radiance surrounds you. You bestow love on all who follow you. You are cloaked in the power of the boundless sea; all of creation is your mantle. Divine mother, most ancient of the gods, hear the call of your loyal devotee and show forth the realm of your unseen children. As the mighty earth contains all of the sparkling jewels craved by man, so too do your gentle hills contain the object of my desire. Bless me with your presence and gather your immortal children around. For I call myself your own and seek to walk among your mysterious worlds."

Sit quietly with the mirror in front of you. You will now call upon some of the most influential faeries by name, in the hopes that others will follow. With each invocation, ring the bell and sip from the chalice.

"I call upon Manannán Mac Lir, the lord of the grey waves, who doth mend the golden chalice with your rapturous breath. What once was broken is now made whole by your divine power. Great bringer of mists, travel to this sacred grove on the wings of the tur-

bulent wind that blows at your command. The brightness of the sun, the terror of thunder, and the lightning's fire move by your hand. May I be graced by the touch of your watery flesh; all the creatures of the ocean depths are contained within you. You are the guide of travelers, the king of storm and sea. You are the defender of the harvest, the shield of all our nourishment. Endless is your generosity, as you assist and protect even those who reject you and fail to pay you tribute. I offer you my cup and my kiss, may yours be mine.

"I call upon the High King and Queen of Faeries; Finvarra and Onagh, whose benevolence is unmatched. Regal and radiant, you guard the secrets of magic and reveal them to your favored companions. Like sacred wine that ages in darkness within the cosseted womb of the oaken barrel, so too do you protect the stores and stock of your faithful attendants. Yours is the strength and swiftness of horses. In the beating of horse's hooves, the powerful rhythm of your happy music is heard. All creatures of the land are bound by your graceful harmony. I implore you to look upon me with favor. I offer you the sweetness of the comb and the vine that is also your blessing to us mortals.

"I call upon Ainé, the Faerie Queen who doth rule all of the prosperity of the earth. Beautiful Ainé, who grants the spark of life by which our blood flows, all abundance is granted through your power. Sweet Ainé of the Wisps, mother of light, who delights in the pleasures of the earth, yours is the melody that inspires the poet and moves the bard to song. Bless your devotee with health, endow me with the spark of vitality that is your essence. Like the golden light that shines through honeyed wine, may the light of your life-giving powers be mine to behold.

"I call upon Queen Medb, Maeve the Faerie Queen and Sovereign of Connacht. Great lady, maker of kings, count me worthy of your brilliant presence. Queen of enchantment who doth preside over the inaugurations of laudable men, deem me one of your royal court. I come before you with sweetness. I come before you with an adoring heart. I come before you with humility. Look favorably upon me and grant me audience with your sparkling attendants. You who are sovereign of the earth, my home, I call you by name to render thin the veil between the worlds that separates us. Let us share this fleeting dance if only for an instant.

"I beckon and welcome all you denizens of the Seelie Court! Your benevolence and kindness has touched my heart. I set delights before you, that you may enjoy the return of the blessings you freely give."

Cut a piece of cake with the athalme or bolline, but do not eat it. Pour a libation into the earth and sit with the mirror before you. Gaze into it steadily, looking for any evidence of faerie presence, such as movements in the grass that cannot be attributed to wind or insects or fleeting lights that do not come from fireflies. The mirror will be especially helpful because faeries will generally shun direct eye contact with humans. They will often appear to disintegrate before your eyes rather than meet your gaze. Remember that faeries are capricious by nature and that sometimes no amount of wooing can coax them into interaction. But it is their very unpredictable nature that many find so intriguing. When you are either satisfied or discouraged enough to leave, release the quarters and leave some wine and cake behind. Chances are that at best, you will have enjoyed a mystical experience and at worst, a peaceful evening surrounded by nature, which in and of itself is a worthwhile endeavor.

Practical Craft
FIRE MAGIC

Fire was considered by many cultures to be a gift from the gods. Whether bestowed by the deities or stolen by mortals, the use of flame in cult practice as protective magic, devotional offering, and instrument of destruction is a recurring reality. From the torture of Prometheus by Zeus' eagle—his punishment for stealing the fire of heaven and distributing it among mortals—to the flames that consumed the sacrificial victims of the druidic conflagrations, fire has been regarded as one of the most potent elements of the gods and an important feature of ritual.

Celtic lore contends that all hearth fires were lit from a single central fire, representing the need fire of the gods, which was typically a fire that burned for three consecutive days. It was believed that a need fire would unify the land, home, and occupants of the property on which it burned, securing and protecting their ownership of hard-won gains. Today, there are many ways to safely use fire as a symbol of devotion, acknowledging its ancient power.

Sacred Flames
The fires of midsummer are an earthly testament to the pinnacle of the ascendancy of the sun. Mirroring the power of

the sun at its peak, the great bonfires and devotional candles lit by the followers of the Wiccan year seek the same end: to align with the divine energy as manifested through the visible culmination of our nearest star. The simple observance of lighting a sacred fire reminds us of the importance of attuning with the season in order to honor the deities and align with ancient practices. Men and women used to run naked through the midsummer flames, believing it would protect them from evil.

If you do not have access to a field where a bonfire would be a reasonable option, and if a candle does not have the significant symbolic weight that you desire, there is another method of creating a representational midsummer blaze. You can combine Epsom salts and rubbing alcohol for a smoke-free and contained altar fire that is suitable for indoor use. You will need these things:

3 tablespoons Epsom salts	*Two bricks*
2 tablespoons rubbing alcohol	*Trivet*
Cauldron, or other fireproof container	

First, consider the placement of your altar. If it is set up next to any curtains or other hanging or draped fabric, move it several feet away. Also check the air circulation of the room. It doesn't make a lot of sense to go to the trouble of moving your altar clear of your draperies or wall hangings if you have a fan on that will blow the flames in that direction anyway.

Use extreme caution and examine the room from many angles to eliminate any potential hazards. Make sure your altar is also clear of any potentially flammable items. This would be a good time to remove and cleanse your altar cloth and sacred tools as a spiritual preparation as well as a practical one. Discard or temporarily remove any dried flowers or pictures that may interfere. Place the bricks side by side on your altar, lying horizontally, not vertically. Place the trivet (or other heat-protective surface) on top of the bricks and your cauldron on top of the trivet. Any heat transferred from the trivet will be absorbed by the bricks, minimizing any significant amount of heat that might affect the surface of your altar. If you are drawn to leap over the flames, set up the fireproofing on the floor instead of the altar and be sure to remove any clothing that has the potential of attracting and feeding the flames!

Measure out the salts into the cauldron and saturate them with the alcohol. Using a besom straw or long kitchen match, ignite the alcohol. Remove the straw or match quickly and blow it out. Alternately, you can use a short match to ignite the flames by striking it and dropping it in the cauldron.

This recipe will produce flames about six to eight inches high after lighting. The flames will gradually wane in size. The entire fire lasts about 15 minutes, making it a nice focal point for a short meditation during a ritual. It does not produce any smoke and only a slight odor that can be offset with incense (burned separately). If you find it necessary to extinguish the fire before it burns out on its own, you can smother it by depriving it of oxygen. This is easily accomplished by placing a metal or ceramic plate over the top of the cauldron or container. The plate should cover the mouth of the container completely to snuff out the fire in a few seconds.

Candle Magic

To recall the sentiment of the need fire, you may find it desirable to burn candles for three consecutive days. Select a candle that has the sufficient burning life (usually indicated on the label by how many hours the flame will last). If you cannot locate a candle that will last at least seventy-two hours, you can compromise by using three twenty-four-hour candles, lighting them consecutively. Choose bright, warm colors, such as red, orange, or yellow (or all three). Carve a solar cross (equal-armed cross within a circle) on the side of the candle with rays extending outward to pay homage to this pinnacle time of dominant light.

Keep the lit candle in an undisturbed location. When you have to leave your altar, let the candles burn in the middle of the bathtub (making sure any shower curtain is pulled back). If you're using shorter life candles, remember to light the next one from the first one, and so on, before the candle burns down in entirety.

By Many Names

Midsummer, Midsummer's Eve, Solestitia, Alban Herium, and Bonfire Night are some of the other names by which the sabbat of Litha is known. The Christianized version of the holiday is known as St. John's Day, which celebrates the birthday of John the Baptist. The modern celebration of the Nativity of Christ near the winter solstice and the birth of John the Baptist near the summer solstice bears an uncanny resemblance to the pivotal exchange of power between the Holly King and the Oak King of paganism.

Season Seven

LUGHNASAD

BETWEEN HOPE AND FEAR

GAZE WESTWARD AND bid hail and farewell to the sun, for the lengthening of nights is apparent now. Journeying south toward the celestial equator, the sun begins to spend less time above the horizon. We are now halfway to autumn. The fruits of summer are abundant as they give way to the grains of the harvest. The first sheaves are cut and lie waiting in the fields. Although the fruits of labor have reached their pinnacle, the results remain unknown. Until the harvest is brought into the home, we do not really know to what extent our hard work has paid off. Themes of hope, belief, and trust dominate the sabbat of Lughnasad, which is also the traditional time for handfastings between beloveds.

Celebrated on August Eve, or August 1, Lughnasad represents the first day of Celtic autumn and the last of the four great fire festivals of the Celtic year. It is also the first of the three annual harvests along with Mabon, the second harvest, and Samhain, the third and final harvest of the year. Typical Lughnasad observances included the gathering of wild berries and the climbing of hills, as well as the visitations of holy wells. The Lughnasad feast typically featured corn and bread baked from new wheat. Lughnasad was also characterized by the selling of livestock and the country fair, replete with festivals, games, and dances. Often, the celebrations would last for weeks, sometimes an entire month beginning in mid-July and commencing through mid-August.

LUGH, THE SUN GOD OF THE ENDING SUMMER

Named for the Celtic deity, Lugh, the sabbat of Lughnasad is a tribute to the first harvest and the beginning of the end of the summer. Most legends attribute Lugh's parentage to the Dagda, the supreme god of the land. As a father-god, the status of the Dagda was grand indeed. His titles include "the Mighty One of Great Knowledge" and "the Good God." Although often described as a primitive deity, the Dagda was the High King of the Tuatha Dé Danaan. It was believed that the Dagda controlled the weather and was responsible for the life of the harvest. His attributes include the cauldron of transformation and a mighty weapon, his club.

Lugh's ancestry portrays him as the grandson of Balor, a Fomorian king with terrible powers. It was revealed to Balor in a prophecy that he would be killed by his own grandson. Attempting to avoid this fate, he imprisoned his daughter Eithne and held her captive so that no man could ever touch her. His strategy was subverted by her lover, Cian, who was able to gain access to Eithne by disguising himself as a woman. Eithne gave birth to triplets, and of the three, only Lugh survived.

Fostered by Manannán and Tailtiu, Lugh approached the Tuatha Dé Danaan at Tara, the high court of the ancient pagan kings, and offered his services. Nuada was hesitant to accept him at first, for there was no skill that Lugh possessed that was not already fulfilled by an individual member of his court. When Lugh challenged the court to consider that he was the only person to have such a diverse mastery of carpentry, smithcraft, weaponry, music, magic, and history, the Tuatha Dé Danaan conceded that Lugh was a most rare and noteworthy individual. They gave him the name *Samildanch*, meaning "the one of many skills." Here was the hero that would lead them to victory against the Fomorians. One of his epithets was "Lámfhoda, or

Lammastide

Lammas, meaning "loaf mass," is another word for Lughnasad. It is derived from *hlaf*, the Saxon word for loaf. The association of Lammastide with bread and grains stems from the gathering of the first harvest, which was often winter wheat and apples. In Scotland, Lammas was a day of accounting; tenant farmers would make a payment to their landlords, often with the first grains of the harvest.

"long arms," which referred to his prowess on the battlefield. It was said that no enemy could escape the reach of his weapons and that his spear would wield itself. He ultimately faced his grandfather on the battlefield and fulfilled the prophecy, driving Balor's evil eye through the back of his head, killing him.

Lugh has been compared to Mercury in the Roman pantheon, in that he is considered a master of arts and a binder of oaths. He is called the "Shining One" and is distinguished by his myriad skills. Some Celtic myths claim that he created the sabbat of Lughnasad as a means of honoring his foster mother, the goddess Tailtiu who died on that day. It has also been suggested that Lugh initiated the festival as a tribute to his two wives. He is considered a guardian of promises and the god of oaths; most likely for this reason his feast day has been associated with vows between lovers and temporary marriages.

Legends and Lore: The Great Assembly

178

In Ireland, it was believed that the Fir Bolgs arrived on the island on August 1, creating the first warrior aristocracy. August 1 was also auspicious because it was the date on which the continental Celtic people held the great Council of the Gauls. A similar gathering, instituted by Lugh, occurred in Ireland on August 1, referred to as the Assembly of Tailtiu. The Roman emperor Augustus used the Council of the Gauls to subjugate the Celts and usurp the worship of Lugh by demanding that the gathering convene in Lyon.

In Irish folklore, Lugh is directly linked to the prosperity of the land through his allegorical marriage to Eriu. Eriu, depicted as a hag, represented the land of Ireland. By her marriage to Lugh, she was transformed into a great beauty. As a personification of the land, her transformation established the power of the god and the sovereignty of Ireland.

Celestial Event
THE PERSEIDS

An amazing celestial event coincides with the season of Lughnasad. Radiating from the constellation Perseus, a spectacular meteor shower known as the Perseid meteor shower dominates the night sky beginning around July 17 and peaking on August 12, continuing to put on an impressive show until August 24. With its theme of hope, there is perhaps no season better suited to wishing upon a shooting star, and the night skies on Lughnasad will be full of them. You can expect sightings of between fifty and 100 meteors each hour.

Several times throughout the course of the year, the Earth's orbit passes through the remaining particles of a defunct comet. It is these particles, called meteoroids, that you are observing. When they enter the Earth's atmosphere, they burn up as meteors. The Perseid meteor shower is one of the most reliable.

The Perseid meteors are often referred to as "the Children of Perseus." Look for the constellation Perseus along the northern horizon. Although meteors can appear in any part of the sky, they will originate from the radiant constellation. The meteor shower is best viewed after midnight, for at this time, the rotation of the earth will allow you to be facing the meteors head on, as opposed to viewing them from behind. The darker the sky, the better. If you can, find a remote area for stargazing, beyond the glare of city lights, which will greatly interfere with your ability to see the meteors. A bright full moon and even a quarter moon can also greatly interfere with the number of meteors that you will be able to see, if any. Choose a new moon night, or if there is not a coinciding new moon, wait until after the moon has set.

As with many of the rituals, spells, and crafts described in this book, patience is paramount. The best way to enjoy a meteor shower is to dress warmly and comfortably, for even the balmiest August day will surrender to the chill of night hours after the sun has departed the horizon. Bring a blanket or a lawn chair, or both. Get comfortable and settle in for an exciting display. Think of all the things that you are hoping will come to pass in the near future as you witness the falling fires from heaven.

180

Astrological Influences
THE REIGN OF LEO AND THE AGE OF NOBILITY

The celestial lion, which first appeared in the night sky on Imbolc, the feast of Brighid, is now lost in the sun's glare as we contemplate Brighid's polar opposite in Lugh. A positive, masculine sign, Leo is the fifth sign of the zodiac and represents responsibility, full maturity, and parenthood. Tropical astrology places the sun in Leo from July 23 until August 22. Moving beyond innocence and adolescence, the sign of Leo beckons us to nurture and take responsibility for our creations.

These ideals correlate to the theme of beginning the harvest at Lughnasad. Having enjoyed being cared for and cherished, the evolving soul now seeks to return that energy to others. The frolics of budding fertility and the excitement of newly discovered sexuality transform into acceptance of the arduous work that sustaining life requires. Powerful goddesses accompany the sun god in the association with Leo. For inspiration, consider the Babylonian goddess Neshtu, known as the lioness, or the lion-headed warrior goddess of the Egyptian pantheon, Sekhmet.

Leo is ruled by the sun, and at Lughnasad, we honor the sun god in his role as the provider of the harvest; the life-giving

Polarity at Lughnasad: The House of the Moon

Although tropical astrology places the sabbat of Lughnasad in Leo, today the sun is actually in the constellation Cancer on the first of August. Ruled by the moon, Cancer can be seen as the energy of polarity commanding contemplation at Lughnasad. In the moon we see the reflected light of the sun, inviting us to reflect on the image of the goddess as well as the god.

rays of the sun enabled the fields to grow. Now it is time for the reaping, and Leo invites us to take measure of our talents and expect success.

The symbology of the lion denotes strength and nobility. The lion is called "king of the beasts," and is a symbol of power as well as responsibility. In folklore, the lion is distinguished more for generosity and mercifulness than ferocity or aggression. Consider the tale of Androcles and the lion, in which the lion spares the life of a man condemned to die in repayment for a previous kindness. Even though he is starving, the lion dares not harm the man who once pulled a painful thorn from his paw. In the fable, "The Lion and the Mouse," Aesop describes a lion who generously spares the life of a little mouse who later returns the kindness shown to him by rescuing the lion in his hour of need, chewing through his bonds and allowing him to escape.

Consider the implications of generosity as they pertain to your own symbolic reaping at Lughnasad. What is the best gift you can give to the world at this time? What are your unique talents, and who helped you develop them? Are you in a position to pass on your knowledge and successful methods to those coming up behind you? Are you willing to share your good fortune, or do you intend to keep the lion's share for yourself? Remember the law of three: That which you send out will be returned to you threefold. By enriching the lives of others or by making the world a better place, you increase your own bounty. Leo invites us to step forward into the light and share the spoils with those who helped us sow the seeds.

Meditation

SAILING ACROSS A SEA OF DREAMS

Follow your heart all the way to the western shore. Chasing the sunset beyond mysterious waters, you find an amazing discovery waiting for you—if, that is, you can overcome a daunting obstacle.

● The corn is high in the fields, waiting to be cut down. Laborers are sharpening their scythes, gleaming crescents of silver honed to perfection in preparation for the awesome task at hand.

● Summer days are growing shorter, and the sunsets seem more brilliant. You want to follow the ebbing rays of light as the horizon claims them. You leave the fields; it is too late for working. The day is done and the night begins to hover, descending upon you through the heavy humid air.

● You enter the forest and follow a narrow winding trail. You wend your way around trees, fallen branches cracking under your feet. A few leaves have already started to fall. The once-lush green foliage of summer is starting to fade ever so slightly. You begin to notice pale yellows as the dense greens fade. You can feel the approach of autumn in the twilight. The dusk seems cooler now than it did just days before.

● Onward you walk, hearing the creatures of the night begin to awaken. You hear footsteps other than your own and you know that the company you keep is with the deer, the raccoons, and opossums. You walk deeper into the forest until the

183

tree line begins to grow sparse. The sky is visible, and you see that the last rays of light are leaving the sky.

● The path widens and changes from soil to sand. You emerge from the dark woods to find yourself on a sandy shore. Several feet away from the trees is the water's edge.

● You watch as the sun drops into the water, then disappears. The remaining light dances upon the surface of the water, shimmering and undulating with the waves as they lap the shore. Before you is a small wooden boat, beached on the sand.

● You are compelled to follow the sun, as if by pursuing the dying rays you could prolong the summer just a little bit longer. You crouch down, grabbing the boat on either side of the bow, and begin to run into the waves.

● The water is sharp and cold as it splashes around your knees. You push off the sandy bottom and jump into the boat. You have no sail, no oars, just a strong intention of your heading. The water is glassy, save for the ripples of the waves.

● You glide across the surface, buoyed by the waves and guided by the wind. You have cast yourself upon the mercy of the elements, and they welcome you gently. You pick up speed and feel the wind in your hair. The air tastes of salt. You hear the cry of a bird overhead as the last gull leaves the sky.

● Around you, a fine mist begins to gather. It surrounds you and impedes your vision. You begin to feel afraid. The light that you craved so dearly has left you. You begin to question your journey. What started as a delightful impulse now seems scary.

● You are alone and adrift on an open sea with no power to move by your own wishes. The mist has gotten so thick that you can scarcely see the bow of the boat. You cannot turn back. You are being pulled along in a journey that you initiated, but that now seems overwhelming with no light to guide you and no end in sight, only a thick fog which is no comfort at all.

● You sail along blindly, moving through great clouds. And suddenly you realize that instead of regretting your choice, which you can't do anything about now, you should instead start to ponder your present circumstance. Is anything hurting you? Actually, no. If anything has indeed happened to you, it has been minor. The source of your discomfort is only that you are right in the middle of the unknown. You left what was familiar. You made a conscious, albeit spontaneous choice to leave solid ground behind in order to aspire to something intangible.

● Whatever your reasons for taking this journey, your sense of adventure has been summoned. The only thing keeping you from enjoying it is your own fear. As soon as you realize this, you smile. And as soon as you smile, the mists begin to part. It is as if the bow of the boat is slicing through the fog, dispelling it as you go. But there is something more at work here. You have stopped. The mists rise and you see that you have run aground.

185

● You plunge feet first into the water, the dissipating mist swirling around you. And you notice that it was neither you nor your vessel that parted the mists. They are disappearing under the light of the sun! How can this be? Is it possible that you chased a sunbeam clear to the other side of the world?

● You can see all the way down to your feet through the clear water. Around your ankles are fantastic aquatic creatures, the likes of which you have never seen. Fish of unimaginable colors dart about; languid seahorses propel themselves through flourishing water plants.

● You step ashore and notice right away that this is no ordinary place. The subtle changes that you noticed in the forest are not present here. The trees are thick with leaves and heavy with fruit. Glistening red apples hang on every silver branch, ripe and large with colors so saturated, they appear like gemstones. Flowers are strewn about. They cover the land with gentle pastels, fiery fuchsias, and shades of blue that rival the sea.

● You look up to the sky. The blazing sun holds its place in the sky, a sky alive with color. You follow the arc of a brilliant rainbow across the sky and you realize that you are on an island. On this enchanted atoll, there is no need for work or toil. The harvest is already gathered, but the fields are still teeming with life.

● You contemplate an ear of corn, so bright and yellow it seems like the light of the sun itself is glowing from within the ripened kernels. You realize that the grain gathered at the harvest holds the promise for next year's crops. And in that instant, you realize where you are.

● You have found the land of all beginnings, the Isle of Apples. You have heard it called by many names. Hy Brasil. Ildathac, Tir na Nog. And you can scarcely believe you are here! Its beauty surpasses even your most incredible imaginings. It is as if you are living inside of a lucid dream. You feel so at peace, so very far beyond the grip of fear that plagued you on your journey. And you relax with the deep understanding that only by overcoming your fear was your passage granted.

You walk across the vibrant land and curl up under a silver tree, the sunlight kissing your face. You close your eyes and take a deep breath. You decide to stay awhile. A land of eternal youth and peace is your home.

LUGHNASAD SPELL TO INFLUENCE AN OUTCOME

As summer dies into fall, we recount the hopes and dreams visualized at the beginning of the year and take into account how often our actions have aligned with our desire. Lughnasad is a time for uncertainty and for embracing the unknown. Its positive aspects embody anticipation of success and the rewards of planning and labor. However, life has taught us that even the best plans may be thwarted, that obstacles often manifest before any great undertaking, and that sometimes the only option is to toss our carefully laid plans out the proverbial window.

The energy of Lughnasad is felt in the time after the test has been taken but before the grade has been assigned. It is the moment after nailing the job interview and hopefully waiting for an offer. It is the sublime first date and the desire for a second. It is putting in a bid for a new home and waiting for it to be accepted. It is sending out invitations for a gathering or an event and waiting for the responses to come in. It is the anticipation of success and the fear of failure that colors Lughnasad in a unique and pensive palette. Use this spell to give you hope as you confront the unknown.

187

You are standing at a crossroads. A great decision lies in front of you. The path you choose will have resounding consequences in your life. How can you discern between choices when you cannot see the future? If you select one plan of action, will you be filled with regret for the road not taken? What if you take no action and leave your destiny to the whims of fate? Does this absolve you should a disappointing outcome manifest?

Making a bold choice even in the face of incomplete information demonstrates a self-confidence and strength of spirit that will no doubt teach you something, even if it is something unexpected. Sometimes you have to rely on your gut instinct, trust your intuition, and give voice to your desire. And that is how we will begin. Think about your current situation and what the best possible resolution or outcome is for you. Reflect on everything that has led you to this point and why you are entitled to your desire. Say it aloud in a clear and concise manner, and back it up with a solid reason why the universe should conform to your will. Your statement must be true. Some examples are these:

188

● "I want this job because I have spent the last three years preparing myself for just this type of opportunity."

● "I want to win this court case because I deserve to be restored of that which was taken from me."

● "I want to win this award because I have put my best effort into this endeavor and I am worthy of recognition."

Of course, your own declaration of desire will be more specific. The examples above are to give you an idea of how to frame things in a direct and supported manner. After saying aloud that which you hope to achieve, write down the exact request on a piece of paper. Use a solar talisman, such as a gold coin (the U.S. Sacagawea dollar works nicely) or a circle of wood or clay with a pinpoint in the middle. Fold the paper over the talisman, and wrap it with an oak leaf. Place the bundle on a circle of yellow cloth and surround it with bay laurel leaves.

Anoint the bundle with High John the Conqueror oil and gather up the ends of the cloth. Tie red yarn around the cloth amulet and secure with seven knots. Breath into the charm, pass it over a candle's flame, sprinkle it with water, and touch it to your pentacle or a dish of salt to charge it with the power of the elements. Carry it with you during the time in between completion of your task and when the results will be revealed. Cast it into a body of moving water when your outcome is due, and anticipate success.

God of the Sun and of Many Loves

189

In addition to his great renown as a hero, warrior, musician, and magician, Lugh is frequently portrayed in Celtic mythology as the perpetual husband. At least four wives have been attributed to Lugh: Eriu, Blodeuwedd, Buí, and Nás are their names. Respectively, the first three represent the earth, flowers, and cattle. Little is known about Nás, although her name appears to be connected with *nasad*, meaning, "assembly," lending some credence to the notion that Lughnasad gatherings were somehow related to the god's desire to honor her.

Ritual

HANDFASTING FOR A YEAR AND A DAY

Handfasting is a temporary marriage between two lovers that typically lasts one year, or one year plus one day. The "year and a day" is based on the ancient calendars that revolved around cycles of lunation rather than the revolution of the earth around the sun. Often, a day would be added to the year when necessary in order to keep the seasonal festivals from traveling.

Also referred to as Teltown marriages, after Tailtiu (Lugh's foster-mother and a place-name as well), handfastings were usually performed on Lughnasad because of its seasonal importance. The long and arduous labor of the harvest was about to begin in earnest and a wife was a precious commodity, especially to a young man about to obligate himself to extended employment away from home.

Since it was common for laborers to spend the entire winter in the vicinity of the harvest work, a young man who took a wife at Lughnasad would be assured of companionship during the cold of winter. Once the work of the harvest began, it left very little time for the pleasures of courtship. This rendered the fall festival an ideal time for making commitments.

At the end of the year, the couples had the choice to renew their handfasting in a second, permanently binding ritual, or alternately, part ways. In addition to the practical reasons for handfasting at Lughnasad, there was a mythical association as well, for Lugh himself took a bride, the beautiful Blodeuwedd, one of the loveliest aspects of the earth goddess. Blodeuwedd was the flower maiden and represented the earth in bloom.

A handfasting can be performed by the couple alone, as the agreement between the two is considered a binding pledge, requiring no other officiant—though an officiant may certainly be included. The first task of any successful ritual or spell is preparation. Enumerate or otherwise express to yourself and to your partner your reasons for the handfasting. What is it, exactly, that you are trying to achieve? Is it a private expression of love, or has the relationship progressed to the point where you wish to make your commitment at least public if not permanent? Are you hoping that it will evolve into a permanent and legal marriage, or are you truly content with the span of a single year, or "a year and a day"? Is this a trial engagement? How long have you known your partner, and are you truly prepared to magically bind yourself to this person? Do you share a common philosophy? Does the handfasting represent your beliefs as a couple, or has one partner only requested it? How do you plan to practically manifest your magical bond? Will you cohabitate with this person? Is exclusivity and monogamy during the handfasting period expected or implied?

Decide before enacting the ritual how you plan to realize your vow. By carefully considering the state of your current relationship as well as your motives for desiring a handfasting, you will be better prepared to navigate the tumultuous waters that partnerships often weather. Be honest with yourself and with your partner about your expectations. By giving voice to your needs and expectations, you will be able to create an emotionally significant ritual experience that will successfully create a unique bond between beloveds. Here you will find a handfasting ritual that can be adapted for a coven or for two individuals.

Treat the occasion with solemnity, showing the proper respect in your bearing and manner of dress. While a handfasting is a joyous occasion, it should also be taken seriously. Wear something special and take pride in your selection. If it is possible, spend the hours preceding the handfasting alone; a balanced relationship involves two whole people coming together in order to experience something larger than themselves. A balanced relationship is not made of two people seeking to fulfill their lives through the presence of another person. Only an individual is responsible for his or her own happiness. As the goddess speaks in her sacred charge, "If what you seek, you do not first find within yourself, you will never find it without." Meditate on this phrase from the charge of the goddess to take in its meaning as it relates to handfasting.

Begin with a simple purification ritual, such as smudging. Burn some sage leaves on a shell or in a ceramic bowl. Set up an altar in the center of the circle and place these things upon it:

192

Athalme	Candle
Chalice	Incense
Gold and silver cord	A stone
Rings	Any other amulets or talismans
Image of the goddess	that represent you as a couple
and/or god	

If you are enacting the ritual without an officiant, take turns wafting the smoke over one another. If an officiant is present, then he or she should do the smudging. If there are any guests or witnesses, they should also be involved in the purification rite. Ask the officiant to smudge each person participating or witnessing the ritual. If there is no officiant, leave the sage burning in a spot outside the circle so that each guest may pass by it and pause for a moment to waft the smoke over themselves.

When all the companions of the circle have gathered, the officiant (priestess or priest) will call the quarters. If there is no officiant, you and your partner can call the quarters. Take turns so that each of you calls in an alternating direction. You can tailor your invocations to reflect your own particular tradition, or you can use some variation of what follows:

Facing east: *"I invoke the spirits of air, you who dwell in the land of sunrise. Gentle spirits of the eastern realm, bear witness to this rite as we exchange the sacred kiss. May the realm of new beginnings bless us with purity and unity. May the placid wind guide us in our chosen path, moving between our bodies to remind us that we are separate, at the same time unifying us in the air we breathe and share. Enfold us in a veil of protection as you descend into this circle. We bid you hail and welcome."*

Facing south: *"I invoke the spirits of fire who dwell in the land of high noon. Fiery spirits of the southern realm, ignite the passion within our souls. May we be blessed by the creative aspects of your nature. May the warm glow of the heart's true love be ours to behold. May we stand within your protected circle of sacred fire,* *that no harm may come to us as long as we stand together. As you descend into this circle, bring us the ardor and devotion that you inspire. We bid you hail and welcome."*

Facing west: *"I invoke the spirits of water who dwell in the land of sunset. Mysterious depths of the western realm, the secrets of the heart's desire are yours. May the sacred chalice of our joy run over, spilling a consecrated libation into the earth. Cleanse us with your encompassing waves, that all doubt be washed away. In your true presence may we accept the gifts of your blessing; renewal, clarity, and trust. We bid you hail and welcome."*

Facing north: *"I invoke the spirits of the earth who dwell in the land of midnight. Strength of mountain, power of the northern realm, lead us to your sacred direction that we know and understand the essence of our true origin. Earth mother, you hold the secrets of the ages. You alone have witnessed the eternal birth of souls. Stand with us firm and true as our souls unite in harmonious accord. Give us your blessing as you descend into this circle; may we be stoic and strong that our bond may hold fast for the time of our choosing. We bid you hail and welcome."*

The next step involves formally invoking the deities and asking for their guidance and blessing as you navigate through your handfasting span. Before enacting the handfasting, you hopefully took some opportunity to explore your own personal mythology as well as the personal mythology of your partner. Learning about each other and the traditions that you each hold with importance will empower you to invoke the deities with which you most resonate. Use what you have learned from each other to craft your invocations. After the calling of the quarters, you (or the officiant) will invoke the deities to represent the divine presence in your lives. There are great love stories in many pantheons. Some deities you may consider calling upon are these:

- Isis and Osiris
- Ishtar and Tammuz
- Inanna and Dumuzi
- Lugh and Brighid
- Aphrodite and Eros

Not all of these divine partnerships are of a goddess/consort dynamic. Isis and Osiris are the supreme deities of the Egyptian pantheon and represent polarity: life and death, husband and wife, brother and sister, sun and moon. Both are extremely powerful, although Isis is considered the more dominant of the two. Ishtar and Tammuz are a goddess-and-consort pair, where the goddess relinquishes her divine power in order to rescue her lover from the underworld. Their story is the triumph of love over death itself, in which the power of love transcends all, even one's own identity, no matter how powerful it may be.

195

Inanna and Dumuzi share a similar dynamic, but Inanna does not rescue Dumuzi from death. She descends into the underworld to witness the funeral rites of the Bull of Heaven. Her sister Ereshkigal tricks her into staying in the Dark City, and she is rescued through the love of her devotees. However, no one can return from the land of the dead unchanged, and to return to earth, Inanna must leave someone in her place.

Dumuzi takes Inanna's place in hell and remains there for six months out of the year. The story of the courtship of Inanna and Dumuzi is one of the most beautiful ever written.

Lugh and Brighid are not consorts, but rather polarities that govern opposite ends of the Celtic year. Brighid represents the bride and the coming of spring, while Lugh represents the husband and the coming of autumn. Paying homage to the turning of the seasons would be a suitable inclusion for a handfasting, as most promises are intended to be kept for the span of a year. Aphrodite and Eros are mother and son. They are connected with sensual beauty and erotic love.

If you are new to Wicca or do not yet have a developed mythology that you resonate with, you can always rely on a more general invocation, such as calling upon the Earth Mother and Sky Father. Same-sex unions can focus on specific aspects of the deity as well. Women might be more comfortable invoking Artemis or Diana, and men may choose to call upon Priapus, or Cernunnos and Pan, the great horned gods of the forest, or any of the numerous Greek deities, such as Poseidon and Zeus, who were known for their amorous and erotic inclusiveness.

Whatever pantheon or dynamic you feel best represents you and your partner, your invocation to deity will contain the five basic components that follow. Use the appropriate language to convey the petition to your chosen deities. You are basically requesting these things:

1. You ask that your chosen deity or deities be present and bear witness to the handfasting.

2. You ask that they grant you both their blessing and their aid.

3. You ask that they use their power to guide you through the storms that will gather and pass.

4. You ask that they see your union as an earthly representation of divine love.

5. You ask that they walk beside you and grant protection for as long as you walk together.

When the goddess and the god have been formally invoked, they may make their presence known through an oracular message. Either the officiant or the couple may receive an oracle and should feel free to speak extemporaneously if the occasion arises. If there is no spontaneous oracle, it would be appropriate to prepare some words that represent the function of spirituality within the relationship.

The couple will then stand together in the center of the gathered circle of friends and draw the sacred caim, a protective circle, on the ground. If the ritual is a private one and no companions are present, the caim should still be marked, and the couple will stand within it. If there is an officiant, the officiant will stand outside the caim. The couple exchanges rings, to be worn on the

By Many Names

Lammas, Lammastide, Laa Lhuanys, Calan Awst, August Eve, and Garland Sunday are some other names by which Lughnasad is known.

fourth finger of the left hand. This placement is symbolic, as it adorns the finger that contains a vein that runs straight to the heart. The ring exchange is also symbolic of sexual availability; it may be accompanied with the words that follow. Women may recite the passage referring to the moon goddess, and men may recite the passage referring to the sun god.

"In honor of the Triple Goddess of the Moon, I join with you in the caim we have created. I offer you this ring as a token and symbol of this pledge."

"In honor of the sun god, I join with you in the caim we have created. I offer you this ring as a shining symbol of the light that love brings to our life."

Next, the couple will cross their arms at the wrists and clasp each other's hands. They (or the officiant) will wrap a colored ribbon or cord around their joined hands and loosely tie the ends. (This is where the expression "tying the knot" is believed to have come from.) Typically, the handfasting cord is made from silver-and-gold-colored thread, representing the moon and the sun. The couple may then recite the following chant to each other, alternating each line for a dramatic effect:

"Moon and sky
Earth and sea
I bind to you
And you to me

Sun and moon
Below and above
I consecrate
Our sacred love
To hold you in my heart's embrace
To know the soul of true love's grace
May our union blessed be
Protected by the Mighty Three
Under sky, on earth and sea
I bind to you
And you to me
Anam cara, friend of my soul
Take all of me for I am whole
I give you my left hand, the hand of the heart
For a year and a day, we shall not part
I give you my right hand, the spirit's hand
Our fates be woven into one strand
Neither to go a separate way
Until the end of the year and a day."

199

The officiant will then give the couple her or his own blessing, such as:

"Blessed be the choice of your heart. May you spend your days
in sweetness. As the sun rises in the east and follows its path against
the sky, may companionship bring you comfort. As the sun sets in
the western sky, may love bring you strength. Take delight in each

*other. At the end of the year, we will meet here again with this same
company to see your vow fulfilled and released. So mote it be."*

All participants should acknowledge the blessing on the
couple and concur, "So mote it be." The officiant removes the
cord and presents it to the couple. The officiant (or the couple)
will then take the athalme and the chalice from the altar. The
couple holds the sacred tools and may speak the following traditional Gardnerian Wiccan recitation:

*"As the athalme is to the lover, so the chalice is to the beloved.
Conjoined, they bring blessings."*

The athalme is placed in the chalice, blade pointing downward, and the chalice is held aloft with heads bowed. Feasting
and merriment may commence. At the conclusion of the festivities, the elements and the directions are released with the same
formality as they were invoked. Thanks are given to the deities,
and all are invited to go forth with divine blessings.

Practical Craft
EDIBLE LAMMAS EFFIGY

As Lammas is a celebration of grains that acknowledges the
waning power of the sun god and the beginning of the end of
summer, it is fitting to observe this holiday by preparing bread
in the shape of a man. Bread is a prototypical food and is sym-

bolic of the life force. In this easy recipe, you will learn how to make an effigy of the god by adapting a classic Irish staple. You will need these things:

Large baking sheet	5 cups unbleached white flour
Large knife	3 teaspoons salt
Large mixing bowl	2 teaspoons baking soda
3 cups whole-wheat flour	3 to 4 cups buttermilk

1. Begin by preheating your oven to 475 degrees. Combine the dry ingredients in the large bowl and mix them together well. Add the buttermilk gradually, mixing it in with a wooden spoon until the mixture is soft. If the dough becomes too sticky, you can add some more of the unbleached flour to absorb the excess buttermilk. Turn the dough out onto a floured board and knead the dough, pushing it into itself with the heels of your hand, folding it over, and turning it a quarter of a turn. Shape it into a disc about three inches thick. Cut the dough in half, and then each half in half again. Take two of the quartered pieces and cut them in half. You should have six pieces of dough, two large and four small. Take the four small pieces and one of the large pieces and pat them each into an oblong shape. Take the last piece and shape it into a ball. The ball will be used for the head of the effigy.

2. Transfer the pieces to the baking sheet and assemble them together. Pinch the ball (the head) to join it to the large oblong shape, which will represent the body. The other four pieces will be the appendages. Pinch them into the body to form arms and legs. With the knife, you can make small slashes

201

to indicate features such as eyes and a mouth and navel if you wish. (You can also reserve additional small pieces of dough with which to fashion other anatomical indications, depending on how explicit you want the effigy to be.) Bless your creation with the following words:

"Blessed be thou creature of earth. By my hands you were formed and made, by magic you are forever changed. I stand in this time of waiting, in this time of wanting, to receive the spiritual and physical nourishment that you offer. In your sacred body is the promise of new life, even as I witness how life does wane. In the setting sun, I see your reflection. In the dying embers of the sacred flame, I see your spirit. You who doth freely give even your own life to be consumed, that others may live, I pay tribute to you with the offering, this effigy of your divine power to nourish and restore. By your grace, may I receive sustenance in body and in spirit. And may the grains that have been reaped one day rise again, for such it has been since time immemorial, and such it will be until the ending of all endings. Blessed be."

3. Bake your creation for 15 minutes at 475 degrees, then turn the heat down to 400 degrees and bake for another 20 to 25 minutes. Remove from the baking sheet and wrap in a clean kitchen towel and allow it to cool. You can test for doneness by tapping on the bottom of the effigy. You should hear a hollow sound in the body. Present your effigy on your altar as a symbolic offering to the goddess and a dark and hearty centerpiece to a Lammas ritual feast.

Season Eight

MABON

THE HARVEST IS HOME

ONCE AGAIN WE BASK in the harmonious balance of light and dark. The sun crosses the celestial equator for the second time this year, only this time heading south. Winter's approach is felt as we notice the shortening of days and the harvest is brought into the home. The light is leaving us, and the sun begins to spend less and less time above the horizon. We measure the fruits of our labor and celebrate the bounty of the harvest as we brace for the coming cold.

The descent of the maiden Persephone reminds us of the covenant between Demeter and death; all that dies shall be reborn. The once lush leaves of the summer trees begin to dry and die. As the life force slowly departs, the palette of the sunset colors the forest in blazing reds, glowing oranges, and bright yellows. Soon, the foliage will reach its peak colors and then fall to the ground to decay and fertilize the soil. The green of the fields is gone, but it is replaced with gold. Mabon represents the second harvest of the year, where the fields are emptied as the barns are filled. It is the flurry of activity as preparations are made, tasks are completed, and success is measured. Mark this time by actualizing fulfillment of your own dreams.

THE AUTUMNAL EQUINOX

Inside the megalithic passage tomb of Knowth, in County Meath in Ireland, the autumn equinox sunlight penetrates the western corridor and travels as far as the bend leading to the inner chamber. The stones along the passageways are adorned with intricate carvings of circles, spirals, and serpentine patterns. While the alignment with the autumn equinox is undisputable, just as with Stonehenge, the reasons for this monument's existence are shrouded in mystery. The hollow hill stands mute, keeping its ancient secrets contained within the carefully stacked stones that have stood for over 5,000 years. The passage tombs of Knowth undoubtedly point to ancient knowledge of the equinox. As part of the Wiccan Wheel of the Year, however, the celebration of the autumnal equinox, ushering in the fall and bringing with it the legends of goddesses from many cultures, is actually modern.

The name *Mabon* comes from a relatively obscure Welsh hero whose name means "son of the mother." His tale is of descent and resurrection, as his legends claim that Mabon was stolen from his mother as an infant and held captive in the underworld. He was ultimately rescued and was considered the oldest living human, for he did not age during his sojourn in the land of the dead. Mabon is sometimes connected with Maponus, a Welsh deity described as a divine youth. He is the son of Modron, an early version of the mother goddess, and is often depicted in sculptures naked and holding a lyre, suggesting a link to the sun god Apollo.

The autumnal equinox is most closely associated with the goddess Demeter, who roams the earth in mourning at the loss of her daughter, Persephone. She comes to the city of Eleusis and serves as a nursemaid to Demophoön, the son of Metaneira and Celeus. Demeter loves this child dearly and seeks to confer on Demophoön the immortality of the gods. She anoints his body with ambrosia and lays his body upon the hearth fire by night, purging him of his mortality.

This desire of the goddess to rescue a beloved male child from the possibility of death echoes the legend of Mabon. A strikingly similar version concerns the goddess Isis. During her search for the body of Osiris, Isis came to the city of Byblos and was entrusted with the care of the baby son of Astarte and Malcandre. Like Demeter, Isis tried to confer immortality upon the boy through a nightly ritual wherein she would hold the baby over the hearth fire. When she was discovered by the queen, who reacted in horror at seeing her child placed on the flames, Isis revealed herself as a goddess and discontinued the bestowal of eternal life upon the boy.

While Demeter attempted to assuage her grief by nursing Demophoön, the pain of losing her daughter caused her to devastate the earth, rendering it barren and devoid of plant life. And when her beloved Persephone was finally restored to her at the command of Zeus, she made restitution for her abandonment of the earth. She bestowed the knowledge of cultivation

Legends and Lore: The Mabinogion

Mabon appears to have an etymological link to the *Mabinogion*, a Welsh mythological text. First translated into English in 1838 by Lady Charlotte Guest, the *Mabinogion* centers on the matrilineal legends of the Children of Dôn, who were the Welsh equivalent of the Tuatha Dé Danaan. The four branches of the *Mabinogion* depict stories of courtship, heroics, enchantment, and power. The first cycle concerns the relationship between Pwyll, the prince of Annwn, and Rhiannon, a goddess associated with birds and horses. The second branch is the story of Bran the Blessed, who sets out to rescue his sister, the imprisoned princess Branwen. Bran and Branwen are the children of Dôn and Llyr and are sometimes referred to as children of the sky. The third branch is the story of Branwen's brother Manawydan, who sets out to locate Pryderi, the son of Pwyll and Rhiannon. Pryderi and Rhiannon disappear in an enchanted white mist that destroys the crops. The final branch of the *Mabinogion* tells the story of the surprising birth of Dylan and Llew Llaw Gyffes, the twin sons of Arianrod, who was unaware of her pregnancy and wrongly swore to her virginity.

upon the mortal man Triptolemus, a prince of Eleusis who is credited with establishing agricultural techniques among men.

The ancient theme of the autumnal equinox was associated with either the dying god or the descent of the maiden goddess into the underworld. The modern correlation of the autumnal equinox with the Welsh demigod Mabon references an aspect of the god as divine youth. We are reminded that in all endings, there are also beginnings and that the fields that are cut down will also one day rise again.

Celestial Event
THE SUMMER TRIANGLE

As you have become accustomed to the summer sky, you have no doubt seen the prominent stars of the Summer Triangle slowly ascending the night sky from the southeast. Now as the autumn dawns, the trio of constellations known as Lyra, Cygnus, and Aquila culminate, reaching the zenith. Each one of these constellations contains a first magnitude star that comprises the stellar grouping that we know as the Summer Triangle. So bright are these three stars, Vega, Deneb, and Altair, that the Summer Triangle is visible even in light-drenched urban areas.

207

At first glance, it is easy to identify this brilliant group of three with the goddess. Three is her sacred number, and you will find no brighter stars in the autumn sky arranged in such a lovely trinity. The constellations of the Summer Triangle, however, have a rich mythology all their own.

Lyra, the Celestial Lyre

The easiest to locate is Vega, the westernmost star of the three. Vega is the first magnitude star in the constellation Lyra. Also known as the Lyre, Lyra is a relatively small constellation that boasts a magnificent association. If such a thing as the music of the spheres truly does exists, it would not be difficult to imagine the heavenly strains emanating from this constellation. The lyre was the instrument of Apollo. He bequeathed it to his son Orpheus, who was so adept and skilled at its playing that even the beasts of the forest would weep at the beauty of his melodies.

The legend of Orpheus is significant at Mabon because, similar to the story of Demeter and Persephone, Orpheus also had to make the dark passage to Hades, the realm of the dead. He went to plead for the return of Eurydice, his beloved wife, who died prematurely. Now, no mortal has ever been able to bargain with death, but the Queen of the Underworld was so moved by Orpheus' music that she persuaded her husband to release Eurydice and restore her to earth.

Hades granted his wife's request with one condition: that Orpheus was not to look back at his wife as he led her up to the land of the living. Orpheus agreed, but as he the last few steps up to the light, he began to sense that perhaps he had been deceived and turned to make sure his bride was there. The last he saw of her was her ghost being spirited away back into the depths of hell, and he knew he had lost her forever. He begged and pleaded with the king and queen to no avail. Gaze overhead and see the sparkling instrument that Orpheus played so well, and think on the story of the man who almost conquered the veil with the beauty of his song.

Cygnus, the Swan

Let your eyes leave Lyra and gaze toward the east. Here, you will find the star Deneb glittering on the tail of the celestial swan. Also referred to as the Northern Cross, the great swan soars south, calling to mind flocks of migrating birds leaving the skies in search of warmer climes before the onset of winter. In Celtic mythology, the role of the swan is magically distinct as an emblem of transmutation. In many legends, children of the gods are turned into swans, some intentionally and othersnot.

One of the most poignant stories is of Angus and Caer. Angus was the son of the goddess Boann and the Dagda. His demeanor earned him the comparison to Eros; indeed, he was thought of as the Celtic Eros. He found himself hopelessly in love with a woman who only appeared to him in a dream. So smitten was he with his dream vision that he refused food and drink, fasting for a year and becoming literally love-starved. Worried that his son might die for love, the Dagda searched for the source of Angus's vision. He gathered together an assemblage of 150 nymphs and challenged Angus to find his true love among them.

Angus recognized her immediately. She was Caer, the swan maiden. Every year at the end of the summer, she would go to Dragon-Mouth, a mythical lake where she and all of her attendants would turn into swans. Angus swore that he too would become a swan if it meant he could win her and marry her. Patiently he waited until the day when the great change was to come. He went to the lake and instantly recognized his beloved once again, for of all the swans, Caer was the whitest and the most beautiful. He called out to her and professed his love. Caer spoke an incantation that changed Angus into a swan as well. Together they flew to his *sidhe,* where they regained their human form and lived together in bliss. As the summer ends and autumn begins, let Cygnus the swan remind you of the power of change and the ability of love to conquer seemingly insurmountable hurdles.

Aquila, the Eagle

The last point on our Summer Triangle is Altair. Farther from the other two, in the direction of the southern horizon, Altair is the first-magnitude star in the constellation Aquila, the celestial eagle. The eagle was the messenger of the gods, and of Zeus in particular. Ancient people strongly associated the eagle with the realm of the gods, believing that the eagle was the only creature that was able to look into the sun without blinking. A symbol of power and courage, the eagle is often called the king of the birds and was thought to be able to travel to heaven and back, far beyond the reach of any mortal man. This belief is perhaps the origin of the ancient Babylonian custom of releasing a captured eagle during the funeral of a prominent king. As the body was cremated, the eagle would take to the skies, symbolizing the flight of the soul from the earthly sphere to the realm of the gods. The eagle was most strongly associated with the sun god. In 1675, the German poet Hohberg wrote:

> *The eagle when in time his feathers fly no more,*
> *Renews, restores himself,*
> *Made young by solar flame.*

One cannot help but call to mind the phoenix when the eagle is described in such a regenerative relationship with the sun. In Greek mythology, Zeus rewarded the eagle with a place in the heavens as a tribute for bringing Ganymede, the object of his desire, to Olympus. As we celebrate the fading of the solar flame, look to the eagle in the night sky to remind you of the pathway between earth and the heavens. The celestial eagle makes his long flight against the night sky, taking with him the waning power of the sun god. When the great eagle appears again, it will be time to celebrate the sun's waxing light.

Astrological Influences
THE REIGN OF VIRGO AND LIBRA

The autumnal equinox is in Virgo, as it has been for thousands of years; however, the scales of Libra were the domain of the equinox when tropical astrology was established. Referred to as "The First Point of Libra," the autumnal equinox marks the halfway point of the sun's path through the zodiac. The rich symbology of both Virgo and Libra resonate equally with the autumnal equinox.

Virgo and the Age of the Elder Mother

Virgo is the sixth sign of the zodiac and represents the point in a soul's evolution where full maturity begins to advance. A mutable earth sign, Virgo is the constancy associated with the solid ground as well as the versatility of its flexible nature. Ruled by Mercury, Virgo invites us to take chances stemming from a place of confidence. Often wrongly associated with Astraea, Virgo is more closely linked to Demeter, goddess of the harvest. Most often depicted holding an ear of corn or a sheaf of wheat, Virgo is the fullness and culmination of the nurturing earth. Under her tutelage, we learn to accept our gifts and hone our skills. In tropical astrology, the sun enters Virgo on August 23 and remains until September 22. Let the energy of Virgo inspire you at the autumnal equinox as you take in the bounty of the harvest and show forth the beauty and power of the goddess in your works.

Libra and the Age of Achievement

While the scales of Libra most often careen wildly, perpetually seeking balance, that balance is found in the autumnal equinox, if only for a moment. The powers of light and dark are equal as the season turns from summer to fall. Libra represents the pinnacle time: the point of the soul's evolution where the focus is on outward manifestation for the last time before turning to introspection.

Like the equinox, Libra is also a turning point. Achievements are measured, like the human heart that is weighed upon the scales of the goddess Ma'at, who sits in judgment of the soul upon the death of the body. The person who would seek passage to the afterlife first stands before Ma'at and places his or her heart upon her scale. Ma'at weighs the person's heart against her sacred feather. If the person's heart is not lighter than her feather, he is not allowed to pass on to the next life. Ruled by Venus, the morning and evening star, Libra exudes justice, intelligence, gentleness, and charm. In tropical astrology, the sun enters Libra on September 23 and remains until October 23. May your heart be as light as a feather as you consider the balancing act of Libra during the time of equal day and equal night.

Meditation
THE ELEUSINIAN MYSTERIES

Nowhere in Greek mythology is there to be found a stronger and more poignant image of the mother than Demeter. A daughter of the titans Cronus and Rhea, Demeter was the embodiment of the earth, the grain mother whose mourning over the loss of her daughter set the cycle of the seasons into motion. Unique among the immortals in her sorrow, Demeter shares a special empathetic bond with her followers.

213

She ordered the establishment of the Eleusinian mysteries at Attica, which became the most famous and widely celebrated cult mysteries in the ancient Greek world. So great was their regard that they were assimilated into Roman observances, and it is believed by some that their influence eventually affected western Christian cultures as well. The Eleusinian mysteries seemed to strike at the heart of universal consciousness, transcending cultural differences through a widely human experience. Dominated by agricultural motifs, the secret rites of the mysteries of Eleusis were an international occasion.

Celebrating mystic initiation, the festival included processions that went from Athens to Eleusis, ritual celebrations, songs, fasting, and prayer. Athenian parents were eager to have their children initiated in the mysteries, as a special place in the afterlife as well as prestige in life was accorded those who underwent the holy rites. So important was the enactment of the Eleusinian Mysteries that each year in September and October a fifty-five-day truce was called in any current wars so that the observance of the festival would not be disturbed.

While no one today knows for certain what the holy rites of Eleusis entailed, their prominence and the sheer number of initiates have gifted us with many specifics that can be honored in modern practice. In his comprehensive mythological and historical compilation *Juno Covella*, Lawrence Durdin-Robertson provides us with details regarding this otherwise elusive mystery cycle. Typically, a candidate for initiation into the greater mysteries was prepared by a year of attending the lesser mysteries. The term *mystery* refers to holy rites and signifies the reverence and dignity of the ceremonial rituals. Set aside some time each night for nine days, beginning nine days before the autumnal equinox, to contemplate the ancient power of the Eleusinian mysteries.

The First Night: The Assembly

On the autumnal equinox, or shortly thereabouts, the initiates and attendants would gather together in preparation for the rites. Carriages drawn by oxen carried a select company of women who held baskets containing emblems and talismans sacred to Demeter, usually barley and wheat, a comb, a mirror, and an effigy of a snake. Set these items upon your altar, and invite some like-minded companions to join with you in a narration of Demeter's myth to honor the rite of *agormos*, the assembly.

The Second Night: To the Sea

The second night is called *halade*, meaning "into the sea." The call would go out for the initiates to gather on the shore of the Corinthian Gulf and bathe in the salt sea to purify themselves. Afterward, they would dress in new clothes made of linen and were considered absolved from past transgressions. Draw yourself a hot bath and add a quarter cup sea salt. Soak and forgive yourself for any regrets you may have.

The Third Night: The Offering

It was customary to offer grains to the goddess. Barley was of particular significance for two main reasons. It was believed that barley was first sown and reaped in a field of Eleusis. Additionally, the kernel of barley resembles the female genitalia, and as such, is considered sacred. Set a bowl of barley upon your altar and contemplate the perfect design of nature on the third night of your meditation.

The Fourth Night: The Procession

On the fourth night, the *kalathion*, the "holy basket of Ceres" was carried in a consecrated cart. In a solemn procession, women followed behind bearing baskets filled with wool, salt, reeds, pomegranates, boughs of ivy, and cakes. A libation was offered to Dionysus, but since Demeter abstained from wine during her mourning, the initiates declined to partake and instead, stayed indoors. You can follow their lead as they followed Demeter's by staying home on the fourth night and avoiding revelry in favor of reverence.

The Fifth Night: Eve of the Holy Night

The fifth night was known as torch day, for on this day the participants would run about carrying flaming torches, offering them to the goddess. This was the eve of the holy night, and was acknowledged with the contrast between light and dark. Set your altar with lighted candles as you contemplate the balance between life and death.

The Sixth Night: The Holy Night

Also called Iacchos, after the son of Demeter who accompanied her in her search for Persephone, the Holy Night must have resembled a procession of spirits. Dressed humbly in clothes associated with pilgrims or beggars, the initiates would retrace Demeter's steps, guided by Hecate and Iacchus. They would pause at the base of a fig tree, and again at a bridge on their way to the Telesterion, the Hall of Initiation. From the bridge, an old woman playing the part of Baubo would heckle them. She would encourage them to lay aside their sorrow for a moment and remember to laugh. During this pause, they would drink a mix of barley, water, and mint from vessels previously carried on their heads. This mixture was the only nourishment that Demeter allowed herself while in mourning.

The procession would continue to the gateway of the temple, and the nocturnal rites would begin within the Temple of Initiation. A great fire was lit within the temple and the priest would call for Kore, beating on a drum. The initiates shared a mystical experience as the presence of the goddess was seen in the flames and felt within their souls. They were then invited to contemplate an ear of corn. The husk was pulled back, revealing the mother and daughter aspect of the goddess. The corn is the mother who nourishes, while the kernels are the seeds of new life, her daughter.

After the nocturnal rites, the initiates were crowned with laurel and declared perfect and regenerated. You can align with this practice by meditating on the ear of corn and contemplating illumination.

The Seventh Day: The Games

The day after the Holy Night was celebrated with sports and games. The victors were rewarded for their prowess with a measure of barley, the grain first grown at Eleusis. Make revelry part of your seventh-day observance. Go out and have fun and eat some grains in Demeter's honor.

The Eighth Day: The Lesser Mysteries

It was held that on the eighth day, the Lesser Mysteries were enacted as a way of preparing Aesculapius, the god of medicine and healing, for participation in the Greater Mysteries.

Recall your own initiation and how you came to the path of the goddess as part of your eighth-day meditation.

The Ninth Day: The Earthen Vessels

The last day of the Eleusinian mysteries involved pouring libations of an unknown sort into the earth. Called the *Plemochoai*, or "pouring of plenty," two great circular vessels, one in the east and the other in the west, were emptied into a crack in the earth. The company was dismissed with blessings that they would carry with them all of their lives, and even into the life beyond death. Initiates practiced sound measures of conduct, displaying virtue in just about every way: religious, moral, politic, and public as well as private dealings. They were believed to be under the special protection of the goddess. At the conclusion of your own observance, water your plants and consider your interaction with the world. Dedicate yourself to self-improvement in order to further align with the blessed and respected initiates from another time.

218

Ritual

A SYMBOLIC HARVEST

On the autumnal equinox, pay homage to the deities of the earth. They are Demeter and Dionysus, the goddess of the earth and the god of the vine. Place upon your altar an ear of corn, a loaf of bread, a bowl of grain, and a chalice of wine. Think of all the gifts of the land as you accept their bounty. Touch each object as you call the quarters and relate each one to the harvest:

"Golden is the ripened corn, like the golden rays of the sun rising in the east. The seeds of new life will be carried to the waiting fields on the breath of the wind. To the east and the spirits of air, we bid you hail and welcome!

"The fire of the south is the same that cooks our food and burns in our hearth. By your blessed flame is the transformation of the wheat into nourishment. We take in your essence, o spirits of the south. And to the spirits of fire, we bid you hail and welcome!

"The fruit of the vine glistens in the setting sun. The sacred chalice holds the gift of the god, and in partaking, we share the libation of joyful measure. To the west and the spirits of water, we bid you hail and welcome.

"The abundance of the goddess is evident in the teeming fields. The harvest of her great body sustains our soul. Behold her gifts of the fruitful earth. To the north and the spirits of earth, we bid you hail and welcome."

Invoke the goddess and the god as you give thanks at the harvest season:

"I invoke the mother goddess Demeter, goddess of corn and grain. Yours is the fullness of the season! We gather at this time of equal day and equal night to pay homage to you for your unending bounty. Bless us with your deep love, for are we not all your children? In your divine embrace, we find our true home.

"I invoke Dionysus, the god of the fruitful vine. Of a mortal mother was born a son divine, and among the gods, he is closest to his followers. God of grace and beauty, o wild and untamed one, fill

us with your ecstasy! You are the promise of the soul's rebirth. We
stand in awe of your reckless nature and in reverence of your power.
Bestow upon us your blessing and your gift. May we be the players
in your divine drama."

Hold the corn aloft and take a bite. After doing so, recite
the following invocation:

"Blessed be the corn of the fields. Such was the beginning of
settled life on earth. Through Triptolemus, Demeter reveals the
secrets of its cultivation. In her golden hair is the silk and the seed
that flows in a river of beautiful abundance."

Hold the bread aloft and break off a piece. Eat it slowly, taking in its texture and flavor. Recite the following:

"The bread of life is humankind's first alchemy. Through the
sacred transformation of the elements are our bodies fed and nour-
ished. The goddess feeds us with spiritual food. May the blessings of
her body be ours. She is with us, she is beside us, she dwells in us."

Hold the chalice aloft, take a sip and recite:

"Blessed be the blood of the god that flows into the fertile earth
as he dies and awaits rebirth. His long sleep begins as the welcom-
ing earth opens to receive him. May we be reminded of his return in
the vine that dies and resurrects. Life is eternal and in each death is
the potential for birth. Through his sacrifice, the land increases."

Take some grains from the bowl and sprinkle them onto the ground. Recite:

"The tending of the fields began as a womanly art. Protected by men, skilled at hunting and fighting, the sowing and reaping was done by feminine hands. May we partake of the legacy of our ancient sisters. May our hands be blessed as we continue the sacred tasks."

Meditate on your successes and gains of the year. Give thanks for all that you have received and allow yourself to mourn for the things not meant to be. If you practice with a coven, share the symbolic harvest of the altar offerings and your achievements with your companions. If you are solitary, enjoy the repast yourself and keep your remembrances alive by recounting them in your book of shadows. When you are ready to conclude, use this passage from *Ranae*, by the Greek poet and playwright Aristophanes to honor the essence of the season:

Let us to the flowery meads repair
With deathless roses blooming
Whose balmy sweets impregn the air
Both hills and dales perfuming
Since Fate benign our choir has joined
We'll trip in mystic measure
In sweetest harmony combined
We'll quaff full draughts of pleasure
For us alone the power of the day
A milder light dispenses

And sheds benign a mellow ray
To cheer our ravished senses
For we beheld the mystic show
And braved Eleusis' dangers
We do and know the deeds we owe
To neighbors, friends, and strangers.

Release the quarters, and give thanks to Demeter and Dionysus. Scatter the remains of the feast for the nocturnal creatures of the woodland and pour a libation of thanks into the blessed earth.

Practical Craft
WEAVING A CORNUCOPIA

Mediterranean in origin, the symbol of the cornucopia was embraced by the Celts. An emblem of fertility, the cornucopia is associated with numerous deities in many pantheons. The Celtic horse goddess, Epona, is often depicted with the cornucopia. Her popularity and power is evidenced in how completely she was assimilated into Roman culture. She is also a goddess of grain and is frequently pictured with a dish of wheat. Embracing this goddess, who represented prestige, the Romans were quick to adopt her symbols, which are representative of abundance, and worship her.

Another Celtic deity who bears the emblem of the cornucopia is also one of the greatest and most ancient of the Celtic gods.

He is Cernunnos, the horned one, the god of the wild woods. His horns link him to the agricultural cycle, for the horns of Cernunnos are the horns of the stag, and not the bull. The horns of the deer are shed in the autumn and sprout in the springtime. Cernunnos represents the forces of nature and prosperity. In sculptures, he is often seen accompanied by the cornucopia.

In the Roman pantheon, the cornucopia is the symbol of Flora and Fortuna. It represents the inexhaustible bounty of the fruits of the earth. In Greece, the horn of plenty was the horn of Amalthea, the foster mother of Zeus. The cornucopia is a perfect symbol of the harvest season. The craft of weaving also makes for a lovely meditation. The cornucopia will be a beautiful centerpiece for your harvest altar.

Most of the materials for weaving a cornucopia can be found in nature. You will need to collect three lengths of vine (wisteria, honeysuckle, grapevine, or any other woody vine would make a good choice), each about two feet long, and ten slender green twigs, about a quarter of an inch thick or less. The twigs should all be about twelve inches long and relatively straight or only slightly curved. You will also need basket reeds, which are available in most craft stores, usually sold by the coil. A single coil will be more than enough to complete this project. The width of the

By Many Names

Mabon, Harvest Home, Alban Elfed, and the First Point of Libra are some of the names by which the autumnal equinox is known.

reed will depend on how thick the twigs are; select a reed size that is no more than half as thick as the twigs, or less. The reeds will need to be soaked prior to weaving or they will not be pliable and will snap. If basket reeds are unavailable, raffia is a good substitute. You can even use brightly colored yarn for a more festive and decorative final product. Whatever you choose, it is the intention behind the craft that will enhance its significance.

Gather your materials and spread them out in front of you. Hold your hands in the invoking gesture as you call to mind you successes and gains of the past year. Begin by tying the three equal lengths of vine together at one end using reeds or yarn, and then braid them. Bring the ends together to form a loop and tie them together.

Now make the frame for the cornucopia by wedging all the twigs through the center of the braid, far enough so that about an inch of each twig protrudes through the other side. The twigs should be equidistant around the circle. Bend the protruding ends over into a right angle. (This is why it is important to select green twigs so that they are supple; dried twigs will snap. You can also soak the twigs prior to assembly in order to make them

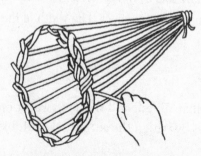

more supple.) Gather the long ends into a point and lash them together with reed or yarn. You can pull the ends slightly off-center to give the frame a horn shape, or leave them as they are to form a cone.

Begin securing the frame by winding reeds or yarn in tight circles completely around the braid. When you come to each of the ten twigs, or "ribs," wrap the reed or yarn twice around the twig where it meets the braid and then continue wrapping

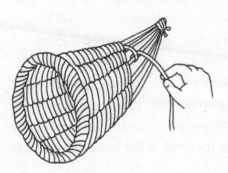

the circle. When you have completed lashing the circle, hide the end of the lasher reed by tucking it inside the rim. This will make the frame sturdier and the rim more attractive.

The reed or yarn that you choose to weave through the cone is called the weaver. Start near the rim with a long length of the weaver and hold it between your thumb and forefinger as you wind it tightly around the first rib, wrapping it in a complete circle. Move on to the next rib, pulling it tight, and circle the weaver around the second rib, and so on. When you have gone around all the ribs and are back at the beginning, tuck the starting end under the weave to hide it.

Continue winding the weaver around the ribs, reciting a song to Adsagsona, the Celtic goddess of spells. Adsagsona is a powerful divinity of magic. Also called "she who seeks out," she is reputed to be able to find the object of any blessing or any curse:

"Adsagsona, weaver of spells, who in all magic and mystery dwells, as I weave your cone of power, I call for your blessing in this hour! May our table ne'er be empty, but blessed by the horn of plenty."

When you reach the tip of the cone, wrap the end of the weaver in a complete circle around the tip, making a loop. Thread the end of the weaver through the loop and pull it tight. Cut the final end to about a quarter inch and tuck it inside the weave. Place the finished cornucopia on your altar and fill it with offerings of the season: small gourds, vegetables, grains, dried herbs, or whatever you feel represents your devotion the best. Enjoy the beauty of the craft you have created and express gratitude for all of the gifts that the goddess has bestowed upon you.

A LUNAR YEAR
AND A DAY

THE ESBATS

THE WICCAN YEAR celebrated today is a solar cycle of fixed holidays. Generally, the sun festivals vary from year to year, while the cross-quarter days are observed on the same dates. And while we have spent much time exploring the orbit of the Earth around the sun and its consequence (that is, the seasons), it would be remiss not to include the influence and role of the moon as it relates to the origin of our concept of time. The moon is the shining wheel of radiant beauty to which we look to personify the goddess in the night sky. Like the seasons, she is constantly changing. She is the reflection of the sun and our closest celestial neighbor. Few heavenly bodies have inspired as much poetry, music, reverence, and awe.

· In addition to the personification of the moon as Goddess, the Wiccan year holds the culminations of the moon's orbit around the Earth as sacred days as well. Full moon days and new moon days are hallowed as esbats, or the lesser holidays celebrated throughout the Wiccan year. Typically used for divination and the partaking of cakes and wine or ale, these significant lunar cycles are another time for covens to gather and enact group ritual together, or for solitaries to deepen themselves and their connection to the goddess through meditation and spellcraft or singular ritual observances.

Perhaps the most poignant esbat ritual is the one known as "drawing down the moon." Drawing down the moon is done by the priestess, or priestess and priest, and it is literally believed to be the power and energy of the goddess descending from the realm of heaven to the earth. The priestess acts as the conduit for the energy and power of the goddess.

In the span of recorded knowledge, the sun-based calendar is a relatively new imposition. Early civilizations first sought to measure time by observing the phases of the moon. Lunar months dictated the year; consequently, the year proved difficult to stabilize for early astronomers. As far back as 5,000 years ago, the Sumerians sought to divide the year into lunar months consisting of thirty days each. The day was further divided into twelve sections, which would correlate with our modern construct of hours, and

Phases of the Moon: Lunation Cycle

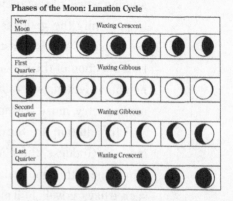

New Moon	Waxing Crescent					
First Quarter	Waxing Gibbous					
Second Quarter	Waning Gibbous					
Last Quarter	Waning Crescent					

each "hour" contained thirty units of measure that correspond with our minutes.

The Egyptians used the alignment of the star Sothis (modern name, Sirius) and the sun to determine the beginning of their 365-day year. They noticed that the Sothis-sun alignment coincided with the flooding of the Nile, a seminal event in their agricultural survival. But because the Egyptians did not have a leap year, the extra one-fourth of a day was accumulated from year to year. This meant that the seasonal festivals were movable feasts instead of fixed—that is, until the Sothic year.

The Sothic year occurred every 1,460 years and was the culmination of all the accumulated fragments of days. On the Sothic year, all of the displaced seasonal festivals were back in alignment. The Egyptian calendar was finally stabilized in 310 B.C. by the emperor Augustus.

The Egyptians were not the only early civilization concerned with the conundrum of defining the year. The Babylonians took the lunar approach by instituting a system of alternating twenty-nine and thirty-day months around 2000 B.C. Like the Celts, they considered the evening to be the beginning of the day and began the month when the first crescent moon was visible in the night sky. The Babylonian year began at the spring equinox and included the occasional extra month to align the lunar calendar with the seasonal festivals.

Later, the Celts would adapt their own calendar of lunation cycles from the Roman calendar. As the invading armies of the Roman Empire encroached, deities as well as concepts of time keeping were assimilated into the Celtic cultural landscape. Found on a shrine to Mars, the Coligny calendar is the only surviving Celtic calendar. Known as the Coligny calendar due to its discovery in the commune of Coligny, France, it is a cycle of twelve lunar months that begins with the full moon in October. Consisting of 355 days, the calendar added an additional month every thirty months in order to reconcile the lunar year to the solar year. It is believed that specific markings on the calendar indicate the agricultural festivals that modern Wiccans celebrate as the sabbats. The thirteen Coligny months are as follows.

Months of the Celtic Year

Samonious	*October–November*
Dumannios	*November–December*
Ruaros	*December–January*
Anagantios	*January–February*
Ogronios	*February–March*
Cutios	*March–April*
Giamonios	*April–May*
Simivisonios	*May–June*
Equos	*June–July*
Elembiuos	*July–August*
Edrimios	*August–September*
Cantlos	*September–October*
Mid Samonious	*Observed every thirtieth month*

The Language of Time
AN EARLY LUNAR CALENDAR ORACLE

An interesting observation made by the esteemed poet and explicator of myth, Robert Graves, links an early alphabet to the lunar year. Graves uncovered remarkable correlations between primitive written language and early attempts at defining the year. The Beth-Luis-Nion tree alphabet is a druidic oracle that was passed down through the centuries. Used for divination, each letter of the alphabet is named after a different tree. Since each tree features prominently in Celtic folklore, Graves made the reasonable assumption that this system, in addition to its oracular uses, also functioned as a seasonal calendar emphasizing tree magic.

The thirteen months of the lunar year along with the corresponding trees and their associated themes are delineated below.

Beth-Luis-Nion Lunar Tree Calendar

Month	Tree	Association
December 24–January 20	Birch	Inception
January 21–February 18	Rowan	Quickening
February 19–March 17	Ash	Power
March 18–April 14	Alder	Protection
April 15–May 12	Willow	Enchantment
May 13–June 9	Hawthorn	Chastity
June 10–July 7	Oak	Triumph

July 8–August 4	Holly	Glory
August 5–September 1	Hazel	Wisdom
September 2–September 29	Vine	Joy and Wrath
September 30–October 27	Ivy	Resurrection
October 28–November 24	Reed	Sovereignty
November 25–December 23	Elder	Death

Astrology and the Moon
THE REALM OF CANCER

Unique among the zodiac signs, Cancer is the only sign ruled by the moon. While other signs may share a common planet of influence (such as Venus with Taurus and Libra, or Mercury with Gemini and Virgo), the celestial crab alone can claim the closest connection to our nearest heavenly body, the one most strongly associated with the goddess.

Cancer is one of the most ancient of named constellations, catalogued by Claudius Ptolemy in A.D. 2. The ecliptic passes through the eye of the crab and every month, the moon glides through the cosmic crab, sometimes occulting its stars as it journeys above and below the ecliptic, never more than five degrees away. This may be the reason that Cancer has been described as "the House of the Moon." To the Egyptians, Cancer was Scarabeus, the beetle of Tem Kephera that holds the ball of the earth in its forelegs. Also known as Sacer, Cancer was depicted as the Egyptian water beetle of immortality in one of the oldest zodiacs known.

Cancer is the fourth sign of the zodiac. A cardinal water sign representing the Age of Maturity, Cancer is strongly associated with the goddess and the connection to the mother aspect. Cancer follows awakening, innocence, and adolescence in the scope of the soul's evolution through the zodiac. Its symbol is the crab. Living along the shoreline, the crab is a creature that is at home between the worlds, for both the water and the land are the crab's domain. Because the crab is known to shed its shell during periods of growth, it has come to represent discarding old ways.

Although the celestial crab has but a minor role in mythology, Cancer is most closely aligned with the goddess Hera. As Hercules was required to defeat the Hydra, a monstrous water snake with many heads, Hera sent a giant crab to interfere with his success. Hercules crushed the crab underfoot and went on to kill the Hydra using fire to cauterize its severed heads so they could not grow back. Loyal to Hera to the death, the crab was rewarded by the goddess with a place in heaven, one of the highest honors that the divinities could afford a semi-immortal or mythological creature. This profound loyalty and attachment to the goddess is a characteristic unique to Cancer among the zodiacs, for although stellar immortality normally is bestowed after death, only in Cancer is the death wrought in direct service of the will of a goddess. The theme of self-sacrifice and maturity further aligns Cancer with the mother aspect, as does its association with the moon. Cancer was known as the Gate of Humanity to the disciples of Plato. It was believed that souls journeyed from

233

heaven, through Cancer, and then to Earth in order to incarnate, endowing Cancer with the role of a sort of spiritual birth canal.

Final Meditation
A YEAR WITH THE MOON GODDESS

As each sabbat has its own deities and observances, so too do the esbats reflect a correlation between aspects of the goddess. Use this meditation, or any part of it, to align your energy with the power of the goddess as she shows her many faces, expressed through many pantheons, during the course of the year.

● The coming cold whispers your name on the gathering wind. In the dark of night, a shining sliver breaks the black expanse above you. Night turns to day and the sliver grows. A crescent glides across the night sky as the preparations for winter are made. This is October, the month of Hathor. In the Sothic year she was regent of the month Athyr. Hers is the crescent crown. And as the moon waxes and grows, so too does her radiance. She is the sacred cow who nourishes the soul. White light pours from the full moon like a river of milk from heaven. This is Hathor's gift to you. Let her blessed milk flow through you, feeding your spirit with her sustaining sweetness.

● The chill deepens and the full moon wanes. This is November, and Cailleach is awakening. She is the veiled one, the woman of winter. Her fingers are the trees bare of leaves. Her voice is the howling wind. Follow her moon of storm and song as you check your winter stores. Cailleach will challenge you; she will leave you cold. She will also strengthen you. When you summon the courage to face the full moon of her veil and stare into the fury of the elements and the unknown, her gifts will be yours. And as she leaves the night sky, leaving you again in perfect darkness, you will come to bless her and welcome her presence when she rises again.

● The snow falls gently in the stillness of the night. You warm yourself in front of a blazing hearth fire and pay homage to the goddess of December. She is Vesta of the everlasting flame. The hearth is her altar, and she beckons you to come closer and be comforted by her glowing warmth. She is the eternal virgin, pure and white as the light of the moon. You feel the heat of her tender love on your cheek. She is the center of your home and the center of your heart. From her leaping and dancing flames come the bonds of sisterhood. Hers is the coldness of space and hers too is the fire that dispels the cold. To embrace Vesta is to rejoice with a glad heart.

● As the radiant wheel of the full moon rises in the January night, let your thoughts turn to Hera, the great queen of Olympus. In her splendid regality, Hera sits on the golden throne of power. She is the sovereign of the month of Gamelion, a time known for sacred weddings. Hera is a queen of civilization, and her rule is as powerful as her wrath. She is the protector of married women and a guardian of marital vows. Hera is a goddess of consequence and is rarely known to ever truly forgive any slight, no matter how small the fault or how penitent the offending party. Pity the unfortunate soul who affronts her honor! In

235

Hera's moon we find the strength to stand up for ourselves; the unwavering resolve that years of subjugation have eroded. Hera was known as the inspirer of the heroes of Argos. Most every home paid homage to Hera's greatness. As you reflect on the cold January moon, remember Hera's resolute ways. Let her inspire you to stand up for yourself, especially in matters of the heart. Her strength is your goddess-given power.

● February comes from the Sabine word *februo,* meaning "to purify." And what better way to describe the sacred month of Brighid, with her purifying fire and healing water? Her voice is sheer poetry, she is the supersensual fire of brilliant words. She is wordsmith, she is metalsmith; the hearth, the forge, and the deep well is her domain. Teacher, healer, the first spark that dispels winter's darkness emanates from her. She is the light of the moon and the light of the mind, the eternal fire that lights the way through the dark. She is one and she is three; a powerful goddess and a trinity. Through her, you will find rebirth.

● Spring is coming, spring is coming! At night you see the silver bow of the goddess of the hunt rise and soar. It is March, and Artemis stalks her game. She embodies swiftness and speed; she is cunning and crafty. Artemis bows to no man and has the skill to topple even the best of them at the hunt. You need not fear her stinging arrows, for just as she adores and protects the creatures of the forest, so too does she protect her devotees. You have seen her power in the ferocity of the bear. You have seen her loveliness in the soft eyes of the doe. She relentlessly pursues her beloved hind, holding it sacred at the same time. Artemis teaches us the thrill of the hunt, she reminds us to be wild and to fear no one! Her full moon reflects the light of her brother, the sun. As her moon wanes, she becomes the elusive game and evades any who would try to capture her. Hers is the indomitable spirit of the maiden. Blessed be her name!

● April comes in a shower of love, and Aphrodite is her name. Beauty personified, she dances on the ephemeral foam of the sea and comes ashore to enchant your dreams with erotic desire. Aphrodite's moon is the fullness of the breast, the voluptuous pearl of the night sky. She is the seducer of men and the object of the heart's longing. The full moon in April shines down upon us in a gentle rain of seductive lust. Aphrodite invites us to revel in our sexuality and embrace our innermost passions. Feel the kiss of her beauteous moonbeam as she alights from heaven above, and allow yourself to experience the pleasures of the flesh, for these are her sacred gifts.

● May erupts with blossoms on every flowering tree. The full moon rises above the tree line, bathing the fragrant jewels of the bough as she climbs through the sky. The diversity of nature is seen in Maia, goddess of May. She is the goddess of new growth and the mother of Mercury. Her voice is the buzzing of the hive, the frenzy of activity and cooperation. She branches out in all directions; it is she who inspires insatiable curiosity. Ingenuity and skill are her hallmarks. Let Maia remind you of your connection to all things; all creatures and people are in harmony within the miracle of her matrix.

● As the honey moon glows in the midsummer nights, June brings us the love of Ishtar. Queen of Heaven, River of Life, Creator of People are among her myriad titles. She is a goddess of love, of strategy, and of battle. Hailed as the Kingmaker, she was the sovereign of Babylon. Most often depicted in the breast-offering pose accompanied by the maxim "The fate of everything she holds in her hands," Ishtar's presence reminds us that bringing forth new life is but one of the many gifts of the goddess. Nurturing and feeding that life so that it can flourish is her true power. Her breasts hold the fate of humanity, and her power is yours. Let Ishtar inspire you to nourish your gifts and talents and those of others as well. Take the sweet honey that is her love and let it radiate outward like her river of life, the river of milk that flows freely from her generous breast. Drink from the deep chalice of her moonlight, and let this fierce goddess of love and strength be your guardian.

● She sprang from her father's head fully grown and fully armed, wielding the mighty hammer that she used to burst forth from her father's skull. She flies with the snow-white owl and she alone wears the Gorgon's head as her aegis. Athena, born from no woman, belongs to no man. She is self-possessed, skillful, and strong; she is queen of the maiden goddesses. Creatrix of the olive tree, she is a defender of cities and a cunning strategist. Call on Athena when you need assistance formulating a plan. The full moon of July belongs to her. May the purity of her light rain upon you like the lightning that flashes in her eyes. Athena is fearless; you can feel her might in the heat of the summer night. Let her power be your inspiration.

● The golden moon of the first harvest rises like a giant lustrous orb, bathing the ripe fields with moonbeams. This is the moon of Ceres, named the goddess of August by the Romans.

Ceres lifts up her skirt and the barley, wheat, oats, rice, corn, and millet cascade in an endless shower. She is the grain mother who ushers in the fall. Her hair is the sunset, her bounty, the mature fields awaiting the reapers. Ceres feeds the world. Her body moves through ours, sustaining us, giving us energy. Feel her radiate from deep within and claim your power. She is your companion as the summer ends, and it is she who will abide with you whenever you hunger for her presence.

September brings us a night as long as its day, and the full moon of Pomona shines upon a wealth of fruits. Hers is the apple that clings to the branch, its color deepening with every day. Hers is the apple that rolls on the ground, so full and heavy with the potency of life that the branch can hold it no longer. Her skin is the tender peach; cherries and raspberries surge through her blood. Apricots glisten in her hair, and the moonlight is reflected in her avocado eyes. Her body is the cornucopia, overflowing with dripping fruits. She offers you her luscious riches, beckoning you to take a bite. Pomona is fullness; she is satisfaction. Walk with Pomona when your dreams have all come true.

The goddess has many faces. She is the night traveler, ever guiding her women through all of time. She is a circle, unending, unbroken. So it has been since the beginning of her cosmic dance. May the grace of the goddess bless you as you walk in her ways. There will be days of sorrow, days for mourning, days for remembering and laughing, days for healing, days for growing, days for planting, nights for frolicking, nights for gathering, nights for dancing, nights for passion, nights for bonfires, for magic and for dreams. Let the sacred wheel unwind and spin.

APPENDIX

Table of Correspondences

Sabbat	Date	Symbol	Direction	Element	Event
Samhain	October 31	Scythe	Northwest	Air	Death
Yule	December 21–22	Bough	North	Earth	Rebirth
Imbolc	February 1	Candle	Northeast	Water	Quickening
Ostara	March 20-21	Egg	East	Air	Growth
Beltane	May 1	Blossom	Southeast	Fire	Consummation
Litha	June 20-21	Fruit	South	Fire	Culmination
Lughnasad	August 1	Sheaf	Southwest	Earth	Decline
Mabon	September 22–23	Cornucopia	West	Water	Harvest

Zodiac Correspondences

Constellation	Glyph	Via Solis: Tropical Astrology	Via Solis: Current Astronomy	Ruling Planet	Planetary Symbol
Aries	♈	March 21-April 20	April 19-May 14	Mars	♂
Taurus	♉	April 21-May 21	May 15-June 21	Venus	♀
Gemini	♊	May 22-June 21	June 21-July 21	Mercury	☿
Cancer	♋	June 22-July22	July 21-Aug. 11	Moon	☽
Leo	♌	July 23-Aug. 22	Aug. 11-Sept. 17	Sun	☉
Virgo	♍	Aug. 23-Sept. 22	Sept. 17-Oct. 31	Mercury	☿
Libra	♎	Sept. 23-Oct. 23	Oct. 31-Nov 23	Venus	♀
Scorpio	♏	Oct. 24-Nov. 21	Nov.23-Nov. 30	Pluto	♅
Sagittarius	♐	Nov. 22-Dec. 21	Dec, 18-Jan. 19	Jupiter	♃
Capricorn	♑	Dec. 22-Jan.20	Jan. 19-Feb. 16	Saturn	♄
Aquarius	♒	Jan. 21-Feb 19	Feb.16-March 12	Uranus	♏
Pisces	♓	Feb. 20-March 20	March 12-April 19	Neptune	♆

Solstices and Equinoxes, 2007–2020

Year	Winter Solstice	Vernal Equinox	Summer Solstice	Autumnal Equinox
2007	December 22	March 21	June 21	September 23
2008	December 21	March 20	June 20	September 22
2009	December 21	March 20	June 21	September 22
2010	December 21	March 20	June 21	September 23
2011	December 22	March 20	June 21	September 23
2012	December 21	March 20	June 20	September 22
2013	December 21	March 20	June 21	September 22
2014	December 21	March 20	June 20	September 23
2015	December 22	March 20	June 20	September 22
2016	December 21	March 20	June 20	September 22
2017	December 21	March 20	June 21	September 22
2018	December 21	March 20	June 21	September 23
2019	December 22	March 20	June 21	September 23
2020	December 21	March 20	June 20	September 22

Astronomical Sabbats

Sabbat	Sun's Position	Constellation
Samhain	15 degrees	Scorpio
Yule	0 degree	Capricorn
Imbolc	15 degrees	Aquarius
Ostara	0 degree	Aries
Beltane	15 degrees	Taurus
Litha	0 degree	Cancer
Lughnasad	15 degrees	Leo
Mabon	0 degree	Libra

Glossary of Terms

asperge   Purification ritual using sprinkled water to bless devotees and dispel negativity.

asterism   A distinct and recognizable pattern of stars that is not itself a larger constellation (for example, the Summer Triangle and the "big dipper" of Ursa Major).

athalme   Double-edged knife with dull or blunted blade, often with a black handle. Used in ceremonial magic.

Beltane   Ancient Irish fire festival honoring fertility. One of the eight sabbats of the Wiccan year, celebrated on May 1.

besom   Witch's broom.

bolline   White-handled knife used for more mundane tasks that the athalme is considered unsuitable for.

Cailleach   Celtic archetypal goddess; the Old Woman of Winter.

caim   Meaning "loop" or "bend," refers to a sacred circle drawn on the ground to separate ritual space from mundane space.

calling the quarters   The act of formally invoking the energy of the four directions and their corresponding elements, usually at the beginning of a ritual.

casting the circle   Preparing a designated space for ritual work, usually includes a purification ritual, calling the quarters, and invoking deity. The boundaries of the circle may be indicated or drawn with an athalme or sword.

cauldron   Black cast-iron vessel representing the womb of the mother goddess. Often used in magic for burnt offerings. Specifically associated with Cerridwen and the Dagda in Celtic mythology.

celestial equator   The projection of the earth's equator against the celestial sphere.

celestial sphere   An imaginary spherical enclosure surrounding the earth; the backdrop against which the stars are seen. Believed in ancient times to actually exist.

chalice   Magical tool representing elemental water and the feminine principle. Often a stemmed glass or goblet.

cone of power   Refers to energy raised during a ritual, usually enhanced by chanting, drumming, or dancing.

copal   Aromatic tree resin, similar to amber.

cord   Usually nine feet long, either red, blue, or white; symbolizes the connection of the witch to the goddess.

daoine sidhe   The faerie folk, or "little people" of Ireland, descended from the Tuatha Dé Danaan.

deosil   Following the direction of the sun; clockwise.

ecliptic   The path that the sun appears to follow across the celestial sphere during the course of a year; the midline of the zodiac.

equinox   The point in time at which the sun crosses the celestial equator.

esbat   A coven meeting other than a sabbat, usually on the full moon.

gleed   A burning coal or ember.

Imbolc   Ancient Irish fire festival honoring the goddess Brighid. One of the eight sabbats of the Wiccan year, celebrated on February 1.

Litha   Germanic name for the celebration of Midsummer. One of the eight sabbats of the Wiccan year, celebrated on or around June 21.

Lughnasad   Ancient Irish fire festival honoring the god Lugh. One of the eight sabbats of the Wiccan year, celebrated on August 1.

Mabon   Modern name for the celebration of the autumnal equinox. One of the eight sabbats of the Wiccan year, celebrated on or around September 22.

Ostara   Modern name for the celebration of the vernal equinox. One of the eight sabbats of the Wiccan year, celebrated on or around March 20.

pentacle   Pentagram enclosed in a circle. Magic tool representing elemental earth. Often made of wood, clay, or metal.

Phoenix   Constellation visible from the Southern Hemisphere, which makes a rare appearance in the Northern Hemisphere at Samhain. Named for the mythical bird that rises from its own ashes once every 500 years.

precession   The subtle shift of the direction of the Earth's axis among the stars.

sabbat   One of the eight seasonal festivals of the Wiccan year.

Samhain   Ancient Irish fire festival honoring the dead. One of the eight sabbats of the Wiccan year, celebrated on October 31.

sidereal year   The time it takes for the earth to revolve around the sun; 365.256 days.

smudging   Native American ceremony involving the burning of sage, sweetgrass, cedar, or any combinations of these herbs in order to purify the psychic energy of an individual or area.

soddag valloo   Ritual cakes, baked and eaten at Samhain.

solstice   The point in time when the sun is at its greatest distance from the celestial equator.

Tropic of Cancer   23.5 degrees latitude north parallel to the equator.

Tropic of Capricorn   23.5 degrees latitude south parallel to the equator.

tropical astrology   The measure of the zodiacal year, beginning when the ecliptic intersects the celestial equator at the vernal equinox.

tropical year   The precise interval of time in between two consecutive vernal equinoxes; 365.242 days.

Tuatha Dé Danaan   Ancient race of Irish gods descended from the goddess Danu. Predecessors of the faeries.

via solis   The apparent path of the sun as viewed from Earth.

wand   Magical tool representing elemental air and the power of the will. Most often made of wood or metal, often the length of the arm from the inner elbow to the tip of the middle finger.

widdershins Counterclockwise movement.

Yule Ancient festival honoring the rebirth of the Sun God. One of the eight sabbats of the Wiccan year, celebrated on or around December 21.

zenith The point in the sky directly overhead.

zodiac The twelve divisions of constellations along the ecliptic, which the sun, moon, and planets move through during the course of a year.

Bibliography

Aveni, Anthony. *Empires of Time*. University Press of Colorado. Boulder, CO. 2002.

Biedermann, Hans. *Dictionary of Symbolism*. Facts on File, New York, NY. 1992.

Briggs, Katharine. *An Encyclopedia of Fairies*. Pantheon Books, New York. 1976.

Buxton, Richard. *The Complete World of Greek Mythology*. Thames & Hudson, New York, NY. 2004.

Child, Francis James. *The English and Scottish Popular Ballads*. Loomis House Press, Northfield, MN. 2005.

Conway, D. J. *Magickal, Mystical Creatures*. Llewellyn Publications, St. Paul, MN. 2001.

Durdin-Robertson, Lawrence. *Juno Covella: Perpetual Calendar of the Fellowship of Isis*. Cesara Publications, Enniscorthy, Ireland. 1982.

Gibilisco, Stan. *Astronomy Demystified*. McGraw Hill, New York, NY. 2003.

Goodman, Linda. *Linda Goodman's Love Signs*. Ballantine Books. New York. 1978.

Graves, Robert. *The White Goddess*. Farrar, Straus, & Giroux. New York. 1966.

Guiley, Rosemary Ellen. *The Encyclopedia of Witches and Witchcraft*. Checkmark Books, New York, NY. 1999.

Hamilton, Edith. *Mythology: Timeless Tales of Gods and Heroes*. Little, Brown, & Co. Boston, MA. 1942.

James, Simon. *The World of the Celts*. Thames and Hudson Ltd. London, England. 1993.

Lewis, James R. *The Astrology Book: The Encyclopedia of Heavenly Influences*. Visible Ink Press, Canton, MI. 2003.

Matthews, John. *The Winter Solstice: The Sacred Traditions of Christmas*. Quest Books, Wheaton, IL. 1998.

McCready, Stuart, ed. *The Discovery of Time*. Sourcebooks, Inc. Naperville, IL. 2001

McMahon Lichte, Shannon. *Irish Wedding Traditions*. Hyperion, New York, NY. 2001

Menzel, Donald H. and Pasachoff, Jay M. *A Field Guide to Stars and Planets*. Houghton Mifflin Co. Boston, MA.1983.

Mercatante, *The Facts on File Encyclopedia of World Mythology and Legend*. Facts on File, Inc. New York, NY. 1988.

Monaghan, Patricia. *The Encyclopedia of Celtic Mythology and Folklore*. Facts on File, Inc. New York, NY. 2004.

Moore, Patrick. *Astronomer's Stars*. W.W. Norton & Co. New York, NY. 1987.

Nissenbaum, Stephen. *The Battle for Christmas*. Vintage Books, New York, NY. 1996.

Parker, Julia and Derek. *Parkers' Astrology*. DK Publishing, New York, NY. 2003.

Raymo, Chet. *365 Starry Nights*. Simon & Schuster, New York, NY. 1982.

Reddy, Francis, and Walz-Chodnacki, Greg. *Celestial Delights: The Best Astronomical Events Through 2010*. Celestial Arts, Berkeley, CA. 2002.

Robertson, Olivia. *Dea: Rites and Mysteries of the Goddess*. Cesara Publications, Enniscorthy, Ireland.

Robertson, Olivia. *Sophia: Cosmic Consciousness of the Goddess*. Cesara Publications, Enniscorthy, Ireland.

Spence, Pamela. *Mad About Mead! Nectar of the Gods*. Llewelyn Publications. St. Paul, MN. 1997.

Squire, Charles. *Celtic Myth and Legend*. New Page Books. Franklin Lakes, NJ. 2001.

Surmach, Yaroslava. *Ukrainian Easter Eggs*. Ukrainian Youth's League of North America, Inc. 1995.

Willis, Roy. *World Mythology*. Henry Holt & Co. New York, NY. 1993

Index